iRODS Primer 2

Integrated Rule-Oriented Data System

Synthesis Lectures on Information Concepts, Retrieval, and Services

Editor

Gary Marchionini, *University of North Carolina, Chapel Hill*

Synthesis Lectures on Information Concepts, Retrieval, and Services publishes short books on topics pertaining to information science and applications of technology to information discovery, production, distribution, and management. Potential topics include: data models, indexing theory and algorithms, classification, information architecture, information economics, privacy and identity, scholarly communication, bibliometrics and webometrics, personal information management, human information behavior, digital libraries, archives and preservation, cultural informatics, information retrieval evaluation, data fusion, relevance feedback, recommendation systems, question answering, natural language processing for retrieval, text summarization, multimedia retrieval, multilingual retrieval, and exploratory search.

iRODS Primer 2: Integrated Rule-Oriented Data System

Hao Xu, Terrell Russell, Jason Coposky, Arcot Rajasekar, Reagan Moore, Antoine de Torcy, Michael Wan, Wayne Shroeder, and Sheau-Yen Chen

ISBN: 978-3-031-01181-8   paperback
ISBN: 978-3-031-02309-5   ebook

DOI 10.1007/978-3-031-02309-5

A Publication in the Springer series
SYNTHESIS LECTURES ON INFORMATION CONCEPTS, RETRIEVAL, AND SERVICES

Lecture #57
Series Editor: Gary Marchionini, *University of North Carolina, Chapel Hill*
Series ISSN
Print 1947-945X   Electronic 1947-9468

iRODS Primer 2

Integrated Rule-Oriented Data System

Hao Xu, Terrell Russell, Jason Coposky, Arcot Rajasekar, Reagan Moore, and Antoine de Torcy
University of North Carolina at Chapel Hill

Michael Wan, Wayne Shroeder, and Sheau-Yen Chen
University of California, San Diego

SYNTHESIS LECTURES ON INFORMATION CONCEPTS, RETRIEVAL, AND SERVICES #57

ABSTRACT

Policy-based data management enables the creation of community-specific collections. Every collection is created for a purpose. The purpose defines the set of properties that will be associated with the collection. The properties are enforced by management policies that control the execution of procedures that are applied whenever data are ingested or accessed. The procedures generate state information that defines the outcome of enforcing the management policy. The state information can be queried to validate assessment criteria and verify that the required collection properties have been conserved. The integrated Rule-Oriented Data System implements the data management framework required to support policy-based data management. Policies are turned into computer actionable Rules. Procedures are composed from a microservice-oriented architecture. The result is a highly extensible and tunable system that can enforce management policies, automate administrative tasks, and periodically validate assessment criteria. iRODS 4.0+ represents a major effort to analyze, harden, and package iRODS for sustainability, modularization, security, and testability. This has led to a fairly significant refactorization of much of the underlying codebase. iRODS has been modularized whereby existing iRODS 3.x functionality has been replaced and provided by small, interoperable plugins. The core is designed to be as immutable as possible and serve as a bus for handling the internal logic of the business of iRODS. Seven major interfaces have been exposed by the core and allow extensibility and separation of functionality into plugins.

KEYWORDS

data life cycle, data grid, digital library, preservation environment, policy-based data management, rule engine, iRODS, metadata catalog, assessment criteria, policies, microservices

Contents

Acknowledgments

This research was supported by:

- NSF ITR 0427196, Constraint-Based Knowledge Systems for Grids, Digital Libraries, and Persistent Archives (2004–2007)

- NARA supplement to NSF SCI 0438741, Cyberinfrastructure; From Vision to Reality—Developing Scalable Data Management Infrastructure in a Data Grid-Enabled Digital Library System (2005–2006)

- NARA supplement to NSF SCI 0438741, Cyberinfrastructure; From Vision to Reality—Research Prototype Persistent Archive Extension (2006–2007)

- NSF SDCI 0721400, SDCI Data Improvement: Data Grids for Community Driven Applications (2007–2010)

- NSF/NARA OCI-0848296, NARA Transcontinental Persistent Archive Prototype (2008–2012)

The views and conclusions contained in this document are those of the authors and should not be interpreted as representing the official policies, either expressed or implied, of the National Archives and Records Administration, the National Science Foundation, or the U.S. Government.

Hao Xu, Terrell Russell, Jason Coposky, Arcot Rajasekar, Reagan Moore, Antoine de Torcy, Michael Wan, Wayne Shroeder, and Sheau-Yen Chen
March 2017

CHAPTER 1

Introduction

Recent decades have seen a rapid rise in collaborative activities in scientific research, and more broadly across many sectors of society. Driven by new information technologies such as the Web as well as the increasing complexity and interdisciplinary nature of today's research problems, from climate change to the world's increasingly integrated economies, the need for technologies, sometimes called "cyberinfrastructure," that enable researchers to collaborate effectively continues to grow rapidly. The Integrated Rule-Oriented Data System (iRODS) is a state-of-the-art software that supports collaborative research, and, more broadly, management, sharing, publication, and long-term preservation of data that are distributed.

A tool for collaboration, iRODS is itself the product of a fruitful collaboration spanning more than two decades among high-performance computing (HPC), preservation, and library communities, whose real-world needs have driven and shaped iRODS development. The computational science and HPC communities are inherently interdisciplinary, generating and using very large data collections distributed across multiple sites and groups. The massive size of these data collections has encouraged development of unique capabilities in iRODS that allow scaling to collections containing petabytes of data and hundreds of millions of files.

The preservation community brings the need for long-term preservation of digital information, a challenging problem that is still an active research area to which iRODS research activities have made significant contributions. Interestingly, there turned out to be significant commonalities in the requirements for preserving digital data in time and collaborative sharing of distributed data collections across space, whether geographic, institutional, disciplinary, etc.

The third community that has contributed to iRODS development is the library community, with expertise in descriptive metadata that is essential for management, discovery, repurposing, as well as controlled sharing and long-term preservation of digital collections.

In collaborating with these communities, iRODS research and development has been characterized by close attention to the practical requirements of a wide range of users, resulting in pioneering architecture and solutions to numerous distributed data challenges that now form the iRODS Data System for managing, sharing, publishing, and preserving today's rapidly growing and increasingly complex digital collections.

iRODS is a software middleware, or "cyberinfrastructure," that organizes distributed data into a sharable collection. The iRODS software is used to implement a *data grid* that assembles data into a logical collection. Properties such as integrity (uncorrupted record), authenticity (linking of provenance information to each record), chain of custody (tracking of location and management controls within the preservation environment), and trustworthiness (sustainability of the records) can be imposed on the logical collection. When data sets are distributed across multiple types of storage systems, across multiple administrative domains, across multiple institutions, and across multiple countries, data grid technology is used to enforce uniform management policies on the assembled collection. The specific challenges addressed by the iRODS Data Grid include the following.

- Management of interactions with storage resources that use different access protocols. The data grid provides mechanisms to map from the actions requested by a client to the protocol required by a specific vendor supplied disk, tape, archive, or object-relational database.

- Support for authentication and authorization across systems that use different identity management systems. The data grid authenticates all access, and authorizes and logs all operations on the files registered into the shared collection.

- Support for uniform management policies across institutions that may have differing access requirements such as different institutional research board approval processes. The policies controlling use, distribution, replication, retention, disposition, authenticity, integrity, and trustworthiness are enforced by the data grid.

- Support for wide-area-network access. To maintain interactive response, network transport is optimized for moving massive files (through parallel input/output (I/O) streams), for moving small files (through encapsulation of the file in the initial data transfer request), for moving large numbers of small files (aggregation into tar files), and for minimizing the amount of data sent over the network (execution of remote procedures such as data subsetting on each storage resource).

In response to these challenges, iRODS is an ongoing research and software development effort to provide software infrastructure solutions that enable collaborative research. The software systems are implemented as middleware that interacts with remote storage systems on behalf of the users. The goal of the iRODS Consortium is to develop generic software that can be used to implement all distributed data management applications, through changing the management policies and procedures. This has been realized by creating a highly extensible software infrastructure that can be modified without requiring the modification of the core software or development of new software code.

This publication describes the data grid technology in Chapter 2, the iRODS architecture in Chapter 3, the Rule-Oriented Programming model in Chapter 4, the iRODS Rule system in Chapter 5, and the iRODS microservices in Chapter 6.

Documentation for iRODS is continually being updated by the growing iRODS open source community on the iRODS website at http://www.irods.org/, covering topics such as installation, how to use iRODS, administration, and development information. The website also contains iRODS-related publications for further reading.

CHAPTER 2

Integrated Rule-Oriented Data System

iRODS is software middleware that manages a highly controlled collection of distributed digital objects, while enforcing user-defined Management Policies across multiple storage locations. The iRODS system is generic software infrastructure that can be tuned to implement any desired data management application, ranging from a Data Grid for sharing data across collaborations, to a digital library for publishing data, to a preservation environment for long-term data retention, to a data processing pipeline, to a system for federating real-time sensor data streams.

The iRODS technology is originally developed by Data Intensive Cyber Environments (DICE) Center at University of North Carolina at Chapel Hill and University of California, San Diego, and is currently developed by the iRODS Consortium, housed within the Renaissance Computing Institute (RENCI) at the University of North Carolina at Chapel Hill.

iRODS 4.0+ represents a major effort to analyze, harden, and package iRODS for sustainability, modularization, security, and testability. This has led to a fairly significant refactorization of much of the underlying codebase. iRODS has been modularized whereby existing iRODS 3.x functionality has been replaced and provided by small, interoperable plugins. The core is designed to be as immutable as possible and serve as a bus for handling the internal logic of the business of iRODS (data storage, policy enforcement, etc.). Seven major interfaces have been exposed by the core and allow extensibility and separation of functionality into plugins. A few plugins are included by default in iRODS to provide a set of base functionality.

The ideas for the iRODS project have existed for a number of years, and became more concrete through the National Science Foundation-funded project, Constraint-Based Knowledge Systems for Grids, Digital Libraries, and Persistent Archives, which began in the Fall of 2004. The development of iRODS was driven by the lessons learned in nearly 10 years of deployment and production use of the DICE Storage Resource Broker (SRB) Data Grid technology and through applications of theories and concepts from a wide range of well-known paradigms from computer science fields such as active databases, program verification, transactional systems, logic programming, business rule systems, constraint-management systems, workflows, and service-oriented architecture. The iRODS Data Grid is an adaptable middleware, in which management policies and management procedures can be dynamically changed without having to rewrite software code.

The iRODS Data Grid expresses management policies as computer actionable rules, and management procedures as sets of remotely executable microservices. The rules control the execution of the microservices. The state information generated by the microservices is stored in a metadata catalog (iCAT). The iRODS Data Grid manages input and output information from the microservices (81 Session Variable Attributes and 109 Persistent State Information Attributes), manages composition of 200+ microservices into Actions that implement the desired management procedures, and enforces 80+ active rules while managing a Distributed Collection. An additional set of eight alternate rules is provided as examples of the tuning of Management Policies to specific institutional requirements. The rules and microservices are targeted toward data management functions needed for a wide variety of data management applications. The open source iRODS Data Grid is highly extensible, supporting dynamic updates to the Rule Base, the incorporation of new microservices, the addition of new Persistent State Information, as well as the use of additional or updated plugins. With the knowledge provided by this document, a reader will be able to add new rules, create new microservices, and build a data management environment that enforces their institutional Management Policies and procedures.

2.1   DATA GRID OVERVIEW

The iRODS technology builds upon the lessons learned from the first generation of data grid technology developed by the DICE group, the SRB. The same basic concepts needed for distributed data management and organization of distributed data into sharable collections that were implemented in the SRB have also been implemented in iRODS.

The DICE SRB Data Grid is a software infrastructure for sharing data and metadata distributed across heterogeneous resources using uniform Application Programming Interfaces (APIs) and Graphical User Interfaces. To provide this functionality, the SRB abstracts key concepts in data management: data object names, and sets of data objects, resources, users, and groups, and provides uniform methods for interacting with the concepts. The SRB hides the underlying physical infrastructure from users by providing global, logical mappings from the digital entities registered into the shared collection to their physical storage locations. Hence, the peculiarities of storage systems and their access methods, the geographic or administrative location of data, and user authentication and authorization across systems, are all hidden from the users. A user can access files from an online file system, near-line tapes, relational databases, sensor data streams, and the Web without having to worry about where they are located, what protocol to use to connect and access the system, and without establishing a separate account or password/certificate to each of the underlying computer systems to gain access. These virtualization mechanisms are implemented in the SRB system by maintaining mappings and profile metadata in a permanent database system called the MCAT Metadata Catalog and by providing integrated data and metadata management, which links the multiple subsystems in a seamless manner.

A key concept is the use of *Logical Name Spaces* to provide uniform names to entities located in different administrative domains and possibly stored on different types of storage resources.

When we use the term Logical Name Space, we mean a set of names that are used by the Data Grid to describe entities. Logical Name Spaces are used to describe the users (user Logical Name Space), the files (file Logical Name Space), and storage resources (resource Logical Name Space). An implication is that the Data Grid must maintain a mapping from the logical names to the names understood by each of the remote storage locations. All operations within the iRODS Data Grid are based on the iRODS Logical Name Spaces. The iRODS system internally performs the mapping to the physical names, and issues operations on behalf of the user at the remote storage location.

Note that the original SRB Data Grid defined three Logical Name Spaces.

1. *Logical names for users.* Each person is known to the Data Grid by a unique name. Each access to the system is authenticated based on either a public key certificate, Kerberos certificates, shared secret, or other token-based authentication (via PAM).

2. *Logical names for files and collections.* The Data Grid supports the logical organization of the distributed files into a hierarchy that can be browsed. A logical collection can be assembled in which files are logically grouped together even though they reside at different locations.

3. *Logical names for storage resources.* The Data Grid can organize resources into hierarchies, and apply operations on those hierarchies. An example is the random resource, in which files are distributed randomly across multiple storage systems. An even more interesting example is the dynamic addition of a new storage resource to a hierarchy, replication of live data to that new storage resource, and then removal of a legacy storage system transparently to the users of the system.

Both the SRB and iRODS Data Grids implement Logical Name Spaces for users, files, and storage resources. The best example to start with is the logical names for files and directories in iRODS: the Data Object and Collection names. Each individual file stored in iRODS has both a logical and physical path and name. The logical names are the collection and dataObject names as they appear in iRODS. These are the names that users can define and see when accessing the iRODS Data Grid.

The iRODS system keeps track of the mapping of these logical names to the physical files (via storage of the mapping in the iCAT Metadata Catalog). Within a single collection, the individual data objects might exist physically on separate file systems and even on separate physical servers. The iRODS system automatically updates the mappings whenever operations are performed on the files, and enables users to access the files (if they have the appropriate authorization) regardless of where the files are physically located.

This is a form of "infrastructure independence," which is essential for managing distributed data. The user or administrator can move the files from one storage file system (Resource) to another, while the logical name the users see remains the same. An old storage system can be replaced by a new one with the physical files migrated to the new storage system. The iRODS system automatically tracks the changes for the users, who continue to reference the files by the persistent and user-definable Logical Name Space.

The following example illustrates this with the iRODS iCommands (Unix-style shell commands that are executed from a command line prompt). Explanatory comments are added after each shell command as a string in parentheses. The command line prompt is "host$" in this example. The commands are shown in *italics*. The output is shown in normal.

```
host$ imkdir t1 (Make a new subcollection t1)
host$ icd t1 (Make t1 the current default working directory)
host$ iput file1 (Store a file into iRODS into the working directory)
host$ ils (Show the files in iRODS, that is the logical file names)

/zz/home/rods/t1:
   file1

host$ ils -l (Show more detail, including the logical resource name)

/zz/home/rods/t1:
   rods 0 demoResc 18351 2017-01-17.12:22 & file1

host$ ils -L (Show more detail, including the physical path where the file
   was stored)

/zz/home/rods/t1:
   rods 0 demoResc 18351 2017-01-17.12:22 & file1
   /scratch/slocal/rods/iRODS/Vault/home/rods/t1/file1
```

The first item on the *ils* output line is the name of the owner of the file (in this case, "rods"). The second item is the replication number, which we further explain below. The third item is the Logical Resource Name. The fourth item is the size of the file in bytes. The fifth item is the date. The sixth item ("&") indicates the file is up-to-date. If a replica is modified, the "&" flag is removed from the out-of-date copies.

In the example above, the iRODS logical name for the file was "file1" and the file was stored in the logical collection "/zz/home/rods/t1". The original physical file name was also "file1". The logical resource name was "demoResc". When iRODS stored a copy of the file onto the storage resource "demoResc", the copy was made at the location:

```
/scratch/slocal/rods/iRODS/Vault/home/rods/t1/file1
```

Any storage location at which an iRODS Server has been installed can be used for the repository through the "-R" command line option. Even though the example below stores "file2" on storage resource "demoRescQe2", both "file1" and "file2" are logically organized into the same logical collection "/zz/home/rods/t1".

```
host$ iput -R demoRescQe2 file2 (Store a file on the ``demoRescQe2''
    vault/host)
host$ ils

/zz/home/rods/t1:
  file1
  file2

host$ ils -l

/zz/home/rods/t1:
  rods 0 demoResc 18351 2017-01-17.12:22 & file1
  rods 0 demoRescQe2 64316 2017-01-17.12:29 & file2

host$ ils -L

/zz/home/rods/t1:
  rods 0 demoResc 18351 2017-01-17.12:22 & file1
    /scratch/slocal/rods/iRODS/Vault/home/rods/t1/file1
  rods 0 demoRescQe2 64316 2017-01-17.12:29 & file2
    /scratch/s1/qe2/iRODS/Vault/home/rods/t1/file2
```

Other operations can be performed on files.

- **Registration** is the creation of iRODS metadata that point to the file without making a copy of the file. The *ireg* command is used instead of *iput* to register a file. In the example below, "file3a" is added to the logical collection. Note that its physical location remains the original file system ("/users/u4/test/file3") and a copy was not made into the iRODS Data Grid.

  ```
  host$ ireg /users/u4/test/file3 /zz/home/rods/t1/file3a
  host$ ils

  /zz/home/rods/t1:
    file1
    file2
    file3a

  host$ ils -l
  ```

```
/zz/home/rods/t1:
   rods 0 demoResc 18351 2017-01-17.12:22 & file1
   rods 0 demoRescQe2 64316 2017-01-17.12:29 & file2
   rods 0 demoResc 10627 2017-01-17.12:31 & file3a

host$ ils -L

/zz/home/rods/t1:
   rods 0 demoResc 18351 2017-01-17.12:22 & file1
      /scratch/slocal/rods/iRODS/Vault/home/rods/t1/file1
   rods 0 demoRescQe2 64316 2017-01-17.12:29 & file2
      /scratch/s1/qe2/iRODS/Vault/home/rods/t1/file2
   rods 0 demoResc 10627 2017-01-17.12:31 & file3a
      /users/u4/test/file3
```

- **Replication** is the creation of multiple copies of a file on different physical resources. Note that the replication is done on a file that is already registered or put into an iRODS logical collection.

```
host$ irepl -R demoRescQe2 file1
host$ ils

/zz/home/rods/t1:
   file1
   file1
   file2
   file3a

host$ ils -l

/zz/home/rods/t1:
   rods 0 demoResc 18351 2017-01-17.12:22 & file1
   rods 1 demoRescQe2 18351 2017-01-17.12:33 & file1
   rods 0 demoRescQe2 64316 2017-01-17.12:29 & file2
   rods 0 demoResc 10627 2017-01-17.12:31 & file3a

host$ ils -L

/zz/home/rods/t1:                              •
```

```
rods 0 demoResc 18351 2017-01-17.12:22 & file1
   /scratch/slocal/rods/iRODS/Vault/home/rods/t1/file1
rods 1 demoRescQe2 18351 2017-01-17.12:33 & file1
   /scratch/s1/qe2/iRODS/Vault/home/rods/t1/file1
rods 0 demoRescQe2 64316 2017-01-17.12:29 & file2
   /scratch/s1/qe2/iRODS/Vault/home/rods/t1/file2
rods 0 demoResc 10627 2017-01-17.12:31 & file3a
   /users/u4/test/file3
```

The replica is indicated by listing the file twice, once for the original file that was stored in the iRODS "demoResc" storage vault, and once for the replica that was stored in the "demoRescQe2" storage vault. The replication number (the second item on the output line) is listed after the name of the owner. Note that the creation dates of the replicas may be different.

A second critical point is that the operations that were performed to put, register, and replicate files within the iRODS Data Grid, were executed under the control of the iRODS Rule Engine. With the default iRODS Rule Language Rule Engine Plugin, the computer actionable rules are read from a Rule Base "core.re" and used to select the procedures that will be executed on each interaction with the system. In the examples above, a default Policy was used to specify how the path name for each file was defined when the file was written to an iRODS storage resource (vault). The specific default rule that was used set the path name under which the file was stored to be the same as the logical path name. This makes it easy to correlate files in storage resources with files in the iRODS logical collection. We explain the syntax of this rule in Section 5.6 on iRODS rules:

```
acSetVaultPathPolicy {
    msiSetGraftPathScheme("no",1);
}
```

When managing large numbers of files, the remote physical storage location may have a limit on the number of files that can be effectively stored in a single directory. When too many files are put into a single physical directory, the file system becomes unresponsive. The iRODS Data Grid provides a procedure (microservice) that can be used to impose two levels of directories and create a random name for the physical path name to the file. We can replace the default rule in the core.re Rule Base for controlling the definition of path names with the following rule:

```
acSetVaultPathPolicy {
    msiSetRandomScheme();
}
```

Once the "core.re" file is changed, all subsequent operations will be controlled by the new set of rules. In the example below, a file is put into the iRODS Data Grid using the new Rule set. We observe that the physical file path is now "…/rods/10/9/file4.1226966101" instead of "…/rods/t1/file4"—that is, the new rule assigns a random number at the end of the physical name and creates and uses two levels of directories ("/10/9/") to keep the number of items in each directory sufficiently low. In some cases, this will provide improved performance and greater capacity.

```
host$ iput file4
host$ ils

/zz/home/rods/t1:
   file1
   file1
   file2
   file3a
   file3b
   file4

host$ ils -l file4

   rods 0 demoResc 27 2017-01-17.15:55 & file4

host$ ils -L file4

   rods 0 demoResc 27 2017-01-17.15:55 & file4
      /scratch/slocal/rods/iRODS/Vault/rods/10/9/file4.1226966101
```

This simple example illustrates why the iRODS Data Grid is viewed as a significant advance over the SRB Data Grid technology. The policy for defining how physical files will be named is under the control of the Data Grid administrator. The SRB Data Grid was a one-size-fits-all system. The policies used in managing the data at the server level were explicitly implemented within the SRB software. Changes to the policies required having to write new SRB software. Also, if a user wanted to perform complex sets of operations on the files, they had to create a script or program that was run at the client level. If a community wanted to perform a different type of operation (say, change the way the access control for files was implemented), they had to change the SRB code with the hope that it did not introduce unintended side effects on other operations.

Requests for such customizable requirements came from the SRB user community itself. For example, one user wanted a feature in which all files in a particular collection should be disabled from being deleted even by the owner or Data Grid administrator, but other collections should behave as before. This kind of collection-level data management Policy is not easily implemented in the SRB Data Grid without a great deal of work. Also, the required software changes are hardwired, making it difficult to reapply the particular SRB Data Grid instance in another project that has a different data deletion policy.

Another example is based on a request to use additional or alternate checks for access controls on sensitive files. This again required specialized coding to implement the capability in the SRB.

A third example occurred when a user wanted to asynchronously replicate (or extract metadata from, or create a lower resolution file from) newly ingested files in a particular collection (or for a specific file type). Implementation of this feature required additional coding and asynchronous scheduling mechanisms not easily done in the SRB.

In iRODS, these types of fine-grained control are possible since every operation within the system can have administrator-defined logic attached, both before and/or after the operation. This abstraction allows iRODS to be significantly more flexible and future-proof.

CHAPTER 3

iRODS Architecture

The iRODS system belongs to a class of middleware that we term *adaptive middleware*. The Adaptive Middleware Architecture (AMA) provides a means for adapting the middleware to meet the needs of the end user community without requiring that they make programming changes. One can view the AMA middleware as a glass box in which users can see how the system works and can tweak the controls to meet their demands. Usually, middleware is the equivalent of a black box for which no changes are programmatically possible to adjust the flow of the operations, except predetermined configuration options that may allow one to set the starting conditions of the middleware.

There are multiple ways to implement an AMA. In our approach, we use a particular methodology that we name *Rule-Oriented Programming* (ROP). The ROP concept is discussed in some detail in Chapter 4.

The iRODS architecture provides a means for customizing data management functions in an easy and declarative fashion using the ROP paradigm. This is accomplished by coding the processes that are being performed in the iRODS Data Grid system as rules (see Chapter 5) that explicitly control the operations that are being performed when an Action is invoked by a particular task. These operations are called microservices (see Chapter 6 on microservices) in iRODS and are C++ functions that are called when executing the rule body. One can modify the flow of tasks when executing the rules by interposing new microservices (or rule invocations) in a given rule or by changing and recompiling the microservice code. Moreover, one can add another rule in the Rule Base for the same task, but with a higher priority so that it is chosen before an existing rule. This preemptive rule will be executed before the original rule. If there is a failure in the execution of any part of this new rule, then the original rule is executed.

The major features of the iRODS architecture include the following.

1. Data Grid Architecture based on a client/server model that controls interactions with distributed storage and compute resources.

2. A Metadata Catalog managed in a database system for maintaining the attributes of data, and state information generated by remote operations.

3. A Rule System for enforcing and executing adaptive rules.

The *iRODS Server* software is installed on each storage system where data will be stored. The remote location of the storage system is normally defined by an Internet Protocol (IP) network addresss. The iRODS Server translates operations into the protocol required by the remote storage system. In addition, a *Rule Engine* is also installed at each storage location. The Rule Engine controls operations performed at that site. The components of the iRODS system include a Client for accessing the Data Grid, Data Grid Servers installed at each storage system, a Rule Engine installed at each storage location, the iCAT Metadata Catalog that stores the persistent state information, and a Rule Base that holds the rules.

The iRODS Data Grid uses persistent state information to record all attributes that are needed about a file, including the name of the file, the location of the file, the owner of the file, a file checksum, a data expiration date, and many others. More than 100 attributes are used by iRODS to manage information about each file. The iRODS Data Grid Servers constitute a peer-to-peer server architecture, in which each server can exchange information with any other iRODS Server.

When a user accesses an iRODS Server, information is exchanged between the iRODS Server and the server that hosts the metadata catalog (catalog_service_provider). The user is authenticated, and the physical location where the user commands will be executed is identified. The user's request is forwarded to the appropriate iRODS Server. The Rule Engine at that location then verifies whether the desired operations can be executed, translates the operations into the protocol required by that type of storage system, and passes the result of the operations back to the iRODS client. Any state information that is generated is registered into the iCAT metadata catalog.

When an iRODS Server is installed at a particular storage location, an iRODS Rule Base is also installed. Each physical server can choose to run a different set of rules, including rules that are specific to the type of storage system at the server's location. Since the Rule Engine at the site where the data reside controls the operations performed on the data, it is possible to implement storage resource-specific policies. For example, a storage system that is used as a data cache may impose a policy on all file put operations that automatically replicates the file to a tape archive.

In order to create a highly extensible architecture, the iRODS Data Grid implements multiple levels of *virtualization*. Clients generate task-initiated event—condition—action workflows. The Actions requested by a client are mapped to sets of standard functions, called microservices. A single client request may invoke the execution of multiple microservices and rules, which are chained together into a workflow.

In turn, the microservices execute standard operations that are performed at the remote storage location. The standard operations are based on the POSIX I/O functions listed in Table 3.1. A given microservice can invoke multiple POSIX I/O calls. Thus, a microservice is intended to simplify expression of procedures by providing an intermediate level of functionality that is easier to chain into a desired Action.

The POSIX I/O calls are then mapped into the protocol required by the storage system through a driver that is written explicitly for that storage system. The Data Grid Middleware comprises the software that maps from the Actions requested by the *client access interface* to the *storage protocol* required by the storage system. This approach means that new access mechanisms

Table 3.1: POSIX I/O commands

Open a file	Open a directory	Seek to a location in file
Create a file	Create a directory	List information about files
Close a file	Close a directory	Display file status
Unlink a file	Remove a directory	
Read a file	Read a directory	Change access permission
Write a file		Force completion of disk write

can be added without having to modify the standard operations performed at the storage systems. Also, new types of storage systems can be integrated into the system by writing new plugins that conform to the storage resource plugin interface without having to modify any of the client-side software or other parts of the server-side software.

The list of POSIX I/O calls includes the ability to do partial reads and writes on a file at a storage device. Since not all storage systems that may be integrated into the Data Grid have this ability (i.e., object storage), caching of files on a second storage system may be necessary.

The iRODS Data Grid effectively implements a *distributed operating system*. Consider the operating system on a laptop. It supports computation, scheduling of applications, data movement, and data storage, and maintains internal tables that track the results of all operations. The iRODS Data Grid also supports computation (execution of microservices), scheduling of rules for deferred execution, data movement between servers, and storage of data, and maintains the persistent state information in a database. The difference is that iRODS implements an environment that uses multiple servers located at distributed sites that are under the control of multiple administrative domains.

For the iRODS Data Grid to work effectively, the data that are moved between the distributed servers have to be linearized for transmission over a network. The remote operations generate Structured Information that is passed between microservices and the Client. The data Structures are specific to each microservice. The requirement that the Structured Information be carefully defined is actually a major advantage, in that it then becomes possible to chain multiple microservices together. The structure of the output from one microservice can be mapped to the required structure for input into another microservice.

The iRODS framework implements multiple mechanisms needed to control the exchange of Structured Information, the execution of the remote microservices, and the interactions between the Rule Base, Rule Engine, Metadata Catalog, and network. The components of the iRODS framework include the following.

- **Data Transport**—Manages parallel I/O streams for moving large files (greater than 32 MB in size) over the network. An optimized transport protocol is used that sends the data with the initial transfer request for small files less than 32 MB in size.

- **Metadata Catalog**—Manages interactions with a relational database to store descriptive metadata and Persistent State Information.

- **Rule Engine**—Manages the computer actionable rules to control selection of Microservices.

- **Execution Control**—Manages scheduling of the microservices that are selected by the Rule Engine. Microservices may be executed at multiple storage locations, or deferred for execution, or executed periodically.

- **Execution Engine**—Manages execution of a microservice. The microservices are written in the "C++" language, and are compiled for a specific operating system. The execution engine manages the input of data to the microservice, and manages the output of data from the microservice.

- **Messaging System**—Manages high-performance message exchange between iRODS Servers. This is required when Structured Information is moved between microservices that are executed at different storage locations.

- **Virtualization Framework**—Coordinates interaction between the framework components.

The mechanisms implemented within the iRODS system are very powerful. They are able to control the execution of workflows at each remote storage location. This linking of multiple remote procedures is called a *server-side workflow* to differentiate it from workflows executed at a compute server under the control of a client (*client-side workflows*). Examples of client-side workflows are grid computing process management systems such as Kepler and Taverna. They typically move data to the computer, process the data, and then move the result to a storage location. The iRODS system effectively moves the computation to the storage location (in the form of a rule that will be executed), applies the rule, and stores the result. This implies that a rule represents a workflow that will be executed to implement a desired Client task.

Two patterns emerge when discussing workflows of varying complexity. These two patterns are "Compute to Data" and "Data to Compute." iRODS can coordinate both of these usage patterns.

The types of workflows that should be executed directly on a storage system have relatively low complexity—a small number of operations compared to the number of bytes in the file. This pattern is called "Compute to Data." If the complexity is sufficiently small, then the amount of time needed to perform the workflow will be less than the time that would have been required to move the file to a compute server. Examples of low-complexity workflows include the extraction of a data subset from a large file, or the parsing of metadata from a file header.

For workflows that have high complexity, it is faster to move the file to a compute server than it is to perform the operations at the remote storage system. This pattern is called "Data to Compute." Examples include workflows where specific software toolchains are installed in a particular location due to licensing or other expenses as well as HPC scenarios where large parallel computation is best coordinated by an external workflow engine.

3.1   VIRTUALIZATION IN IRODS

iRODS provides a new abstraction for data management processes and policies (using the logical rule paradigm) in much the same manner that the SRB provided new abstractions for data objects, collections, resources, users, and metadata. iRODS characterizes the Management Policies that are needed to enforce *authenticity*, *integrity*, *chain of custody*, *access restrictions*, *data placement*, and *data presentation*, and to automate the application of Policies for services such as administration, authentication, authorization, auditing, and accounting, as well as data management policies for retention, disposition, replication, distribution, pre- and post-processing and metadata extraction, and loading. The Management Policies are mapped onto computer actionable rules that control the execution of all data management operations. iRODS can be seen as supporting four types of virtualization beyond those supported by a first-generation Data Grid such as the SRB.

- **Workflow virtualization**. This is the ability to manage the execution of a workflow that is distributed across multiple compute resources. The management of the workflow execution is done independently of the compute resources where the workflow components are executed. This requires the ability to manage the scheduling of the executing jobs and the tracking of their completion status. iRODS implements the concept of workflows through chaining of microservices within nested rule sets and through using shared logical variables that control the workflow. The microservices can share information (output from one microservice used as input to the next microservice) through structures in memory, or by transmission over a network. To send complex structures to a remote server, the structures are serialized (turned into a linear sequence of bytes) by packing routines, and then turned back into the desired structure by unpacking routines at the remote location.

- **Management policy virtualization**. This is the expression of Management Policies as rules that can be implemented independently of the choice of remote storage system. The Policies control what happens within the data grid. A user request is interpreted as a set of tasks that need to be executed. Each task initiates a set of event—condition—actions. Before an action is executed, a pre-process management policy is checked for operations that should be performed. A typical operation is checking for permissions needed to execute the action. Once the action is completed, a post-process management policy is checked for additional operations to perform. An example is creating a thumbnail image on ingestion of a jpeg image.

  We characterize Management Policies in terms of *policy attributes* that control desired outcomes. Consider a policy to minimize risk of data loss. A policy attribute is the number of replicas that will be made for each file within the data grid to minimize risk of data loss. The integrity policy attribute is the "number of replicas." For each desired outcome, rules are defined that control the execution of the standard remote operations. On each rule application, Persistent State Information is generated that describes the result of the remote operation. Consistency rules (or assessment criteria) can be implemented that verify that the remote operation outcomes comply with the Policy Attributes. Rule-based data management infrastructure makes it possible to express Management Policies as rules and define the outcome of the application of each Management Policy in terms of updates to the Persistent State Information. iRODS applies the concept of transactional rules using datalog-type Event—Condition—Action rules working with persistent shared metadata. iRODS implements traditional ACID (Atomicity, Consistency, Isolation, Durability) database properties.

- **Service virtualization**. The operations that are performed by rule-based data management systems can be encapsulated in microservices. A Logical Name Space can be constructed for the microservices that makes it possible to name, organize, and upgrade microservices without having to change the Management Policies. This is one of the key capabilities needed to manage versions of microservices, and enable a system to execute correctly while the microservices are being upgraded. iRODS microservices are constructed on the concepts of well-defined input—output properties, consistency verification, and roll-back properties for error recovery. The iRODS microservices provide a compositional framework realized at runtime.

- **Rule virtualization**. This is a Logical Name Space that allows the rules to be named, organized in sets, and versioned. A Logical Name Space for rules enables the evolution of the rules themselves.

3.2   iRODS COMPONENTS

The iRODS system consists of iRODS Servers that are installed at each storage location, a central iRODS Metadata Catalog or iCAT, and Clients. The iRODS Server contains both the plugin that issues the local storage resource protocol and the iRODS Rule Engine that controls operations performed at the storage location.

Client libraries are available in C, Java, Python, and most recently, Go. These client library interfaces send messages over the network to an iRODS Server. The server interacts with the iRODS iCAT Metadata Catalog to validate the user identity, and authorize the requested operation. The location where the operation will be performed is identified, and the operation request is forwarded to the appropriate remote storage location. The Rule Engine at the storage location selects the rules to invoke (Rule Invoker) from the Rule Base, retrieves current state information as needed from the Configuration files and the Metadata Persistent Repository, stores the current state information in a Session memory, and then invokes the microservices specified by the rules.

As rules, microservices, resources, and metadata are changed, the consistency of the new system must be verified. The architecture design allows for the execution of consistency Modules to verify that the new system is compliant with selected properties of the old system.

The Data Grid Administrator manages and designs the rules used by iRODS, and executes administrative functions through the icommand `iadmin`. The specific administrative commands can be listed by typing

```
iadmin -h
```

Interaction with the storage location is done through a storage resource plugin that translates requests to the protocol of the specific storage device. This makes it possible to store data in a wide variety of types of storage systems, including disks, tape, and object storage.

3.3   USER ENVIRONMENT VARIABLES

Information that defines the preferred user environment is maintained in environment variables that are stored on the user's computer. The Environment Variables specify the default data grid that will be accessed, and properties about the user's default collection.

Each iRODS Data Grid requires a metadata catalog (iCAT) that is managed as an instance within a database. Since databases can manage multiple instances, we assign a unique port number to each instance. The iRODS Data Grid is therefore completely specified by:

irodsHost : irodsZone : irodsPort

3.4   CONFIGURATION FILES

The following configuration files control nearly all aspects of how an iRODS deployment functions. All JSON files validate against the configuration schemas in each installation.

3.4.1   ~/.odbc.ini

This file, in the home directory of the unix service account (default "irods"), defines the unixODBC connection details needed for the iCommands to communicate with the iCAT database. This file was created by the installer package and probably should not be changed.

3.4.2   ~/.irods/.irodsA

This scrambled password file is saved after an `iinit` is run. If this file does not exist, then each iCommand will prompt for a password before authenticating with the iRODS server. If this file does exist, then each iCommand will read this file and use the contents as a cached password token and skip the password prompt. This file can be deleted manually or can be removed by running `iexit full`.

3.4.3   /etc/irods/server_config.json

This file defines the behavior of the server Agent that answers individual requests coming into iRODS. It is created and populated by the installer package.

This file contains the following top level entries:

- `advanced_settings` (required) — Contains subtle network and password related variables. These values should be changed only in concert with all connecting clients and other servers in the Zone.

  - `default_number_of_transfer_threads` (required) (default 4) — The number of threads enabled when parallel transfer is invoked.

  - `default_temporary_password_lifetime_in_seconds` (required) (default 120) — The number of seconds a server-side temporary password is good.

  - `maximum_number_of_concurrent_rule_engine_server_processes` (required) (default 4)

  - `maximum_size_for_single_buffer_in_megabytes` (required) (default 32)

  - `maximum_temporary_password_lifetime_in_seconds` (required) (default 1000)

  - `transfer_buffer_size_for_parallel_transfer_in_megabytes` (required) (default 4)

  - `transfer_chunk_size_for_parallel_transfer_in_megabytes` (required) (default 40)

- `default_dir_mode` (required) (default "0750") — The unix filesystem octal mode for a newly created directory within a resource vault

- `default_file_mode` (required) (default "0600") — The unix filesystem octal mode for a newly created file within a resource vault

- `default_hash_scheme` (required) (default "SHA256") — The hash scheme used for file integrity checking: MD5 or SHA256

- `default_resource_directory` (optional) — The default Vault directory for the initial resource on server installation

- `default_resource_name` (optional) — The name of the initial resource on server installation

- `environment_variables` (required) — Contains a set of key/value properties of the form VARIABLE=VALUE such as "ORACLE_HOME=/full/path" from the server's environment. Can be empty.

- `federation` (required) — Contains an array of objects which each contain the parameters necessary for federating with another grid. The array can be empty, but if an object exists, it must contain the following properties:

    - `catalog_provider_hosts` (required) — An array of hostnames of the catalog service providers in the federated zone.

    - `zone_name` (required) — The name of the federated zone.

    - `zone_key` (required) — The shared authentication secret of the federated zone.

    - `negotiation_key` (required) — The 32-byte encryption key of the federated zone.

- `catalog_provider_hosts` (required) — An array of fully qualified domain names of this Zone's catalog service provider

- `catalog_service_role` (required) — The role of this server, either "provider" or "consumer"

- `kerberos_name` (optional) — Kerberos Distinguished Name for KRB and GSI authentication

- `match_hash_policy` (required) (default "compatible") — Indicates to iRODS whether to use the hash used by the client or the data at rest, or to force the use of the default hash scheme: strict or compatible

- `negotiation_key` (required) — A 32-byte encryption key shared by the zone for use in the advanced negotiation handshake at the beginning of an iRODS client connection

- `pam_no_extend` (optional) — Set PAM password lifetime: 8 hours or 2 weeks, either true or false

- `pam_password_length` (optional) — Maximum length of a PAM password

- `pam_password_max_time` (optional) — Maximum allowed PAM password lifetime

- `pam_password_min_time` (optional) — Minimum allowed PAM password lifetime

- `re_data_variable_mapping_set` (required) — An array of file names comprising the list of data to variable mappings used by the rule engine, for example: { "filename": "core" } which references "core.dvm"

- `re_function_name_mapping_set` (required) — An array of file names comprising the list of function name map used by the rule engine, for example: { "filename": "core" } which references "core.fnm"

- `re_rulebase_set` (required) — This is an array of file names comprising the list of rule files used by the rule engine, for example: { "filename": "core" } which references "core.re." This array is ordered as the order of the rule files affects which (multiply) matching rule would fire first.

- `schema_validation_base_uri` (required) — The URI against which the iRODS server configuration is validated. By default, this will be a local directory which includes the configuration schema. It can be set to any http(s) or file:/// endpoint as long as that endpoint has a copy of the irods_schema_configuration repository. This variable allows a clone of the git repository to live behind an organizational firewall, but still perform its duty as a preflight check on the configuration settings for the entire server.

- `server_control_plane_encryption_algorithm` (required) — The algorithm used to encrypt the control plane communications. This must be the same across all iRODS servers in a Zone. (default "AES-256-CBC")

- `server_control_plane_encryption_num_hash_rounds` (required) (default 16) — The number of hash rounds used in the control plane communications. This must be the same across all iRODS servers in a Zone.

- `server_control_plane_key` (required) — The encryption key required for communicating with the iRODS grid control plane. Must be 32 bytes long. This must be the same across all iRODS servers in a Zone.

- `server_control_plane_port` (required) (default 1248) — The port on which the control plane operates. This must be the same across all iRODS servers in a Zone.

- `server_control_plane_timeout_milliseconds` (required) (default 10000) — The amount of time before a control plane operation will timeout

- `server_port_range_start` (required) (default 20000) — The beginning of the port range available for parallel transfers. This must be the same across all iRODS servers in a Zone.

- `server_port_range_end` (required) (default 20199) — The end of the port range available for parallel transfers. This must be the same across all iRODS servers in a Zone.

- `zone_auth_scheme` (required) — The authentication scheme used by the zone_user: native, PAM, KRB, or GSI

- `zone_key` (required) — The shared secret used for authentication and identification of server-to-server communication. This can be a string of any length, excluding the use of hyphens, for historical purposes. This must be the same across all iRODS servers in a Zone.

- `zone_name` (required) — The name of the Zone in which the server participates. This must be the same across all iRODS servers in a Zone.

- zone_port (required) (default 1247) — The main port used by the Zone for communication. This must be the same across all iRODS servers in a Zone.

- zone_user (required) — The name of the rodsadmin user running this iRODS instance.

Servers in the catalog provider role have the following additional top level entries related to the database connection:

- catalog_database_type (required) — The type of database iRODS is using for the iCAT, either "postgres," "mysql," or "oracle".

- db_host (required) — The hostname of the database server (can be localhost).

- db_odbc_type (required) — The ODBC type, usually "unix".

- db_password (required) — The password for the db_username to connect to the db_name.

- db_port (required) — The port on which the database server is listening.

- db_name (required) — The name of the database used as the iCAT.

- db_username (required) — The database user name.

3.4.4   ~/.irods/irods_environment.json

This is the main iRODS configuration file defining the iRODS environment. Any changes are effective immediately since iCommands reload their environment on every execution.

A client environment file contains the following minimum set of top-level entries.

- irods_host (required) — A fully qualified domain name for the given iRODS server.

- irods_port (required) — The port number for the given iRODS Zone.

- irods_user_name (required) — The username within iRODS for this account.

- irods_zone_name (required) — The name of the iRODS Zone.

A service account environment file contains all of the client environment entries in addition to the following top-level entries.

- irods_authentication_file (optional) — Fully qualified path to a file holding the credentials of an authenticated iRODS user.

- irods_authentication_scheme (optional) — This user's iRODS authentication method, currently: "pam," "krb," "gsi," or "native".

- irods_client_server_negotiation (required) — Set to "request_server_negotiation" indicating advanced negotiation is desired, for use in enabling SSL and other technologies.

- `irods_client_server_policy` (required) — "CS_NEG_REFUSE" for no SSL, "CS_NEG_REQUIRE" to demand SSL, or "CS_NEG_DONT_CARE" to allow the server to decide.

- `irods_control_plane_port` (optional) — The port on which the control plane operates.

- `irods_control_plane_key` (optional) — The encryption key required for communicating with the iRODS grid control plane.

- `irods_cwd` (required) — The current working directory within iRODS.

- `irods_debug` (optional) — Desired verbosity of the debug logging level.

- `irods_default_hash_scheme` (required) — Currently either MD5 or SHA256.

- `irods_default_resource` (required) — The name of the resource used for iRODS operations if one is not specified.

- `irods_encryption_algorithm` (required) — EVP-supplied encryption algorithm for parallel transfer encryption.

- `irods_encryption_key_size` (required) — Key size for parallel transfer encryption.

- `irods_encryption_num_hash_rounds` (required) — Number of hash rounds for parallel transfer encryption.

- `irods_encryption_salt_size` (required) — Salt size for parallel transfer encryption.

- `irods_gsi_server_dn` (optional) — The Distinguished Name of the GSI Server.

- `irods_home` (required) — The home directory within the iRODS Zone for a given user.

- `irods_log_level` (optional) — Desired verbosity of the iRODS logging.

- `irods_match_hash_policy` (required) — Use "strict" to refuse defaulting to another scheme or "compatible" for supporting alternate schemes.

- `irods_plugins_home` (optional) — Directory to use for the client side plugins (useful when Distributing iCommands to Users).

- `irods_ssl_ca_certificate_file` (optional) — Location of a file of trusted CA certificates in PEM format. Note that the certificates in this file are used in conjunction with the system default trusted certificates.

- `irods_ssl_ca_certificate_path` (optional) — Location of a directory containing CA certificates in PEM format. The files each contain one CA certificate. The files are looked up by the CA subject name hash value, which must hence be available. If more than one CA certificate with the same name hash value exist, the extension must be different (e.g., 9d66eef0.0, 9d66eef0.1 etc.). The search is performed in the ordering of the extension number, regardless of other properties of the certificates. Use the "c_rehash" utility to create the necessary links.

- `irods_ssl_certificate_chain_file` (optional) — The file containing the server's certificate chain. The certificates must be in PEM format and must be sorted starting with the subject's certificate (actual client or server certificate), followed by intermediate CA certificates if applicable, and ending at the highest level (root) CA.

- `irods_ssl_certificate_key_file` (optional) — Private key corresponding to the server's certificate in the certificate chain file.

- `irods_ssl_dh_params_file` (optional) — The Diffie-Hellman parameter file location.

- `irods_ssl_verify_server` (optional) — What level of server certificate-based authentication to perform. "none" means not to perform any authentication at all. "cert" means to verify the certificate validity (i.e., that it was signed by a trusted CA). "hostname" means to validate the certificate and to verify that the irods_host's FQDN matches either the common name or one of the subjectAltNames of the certificate. "hostname" is the default setting.

To use an environment file other than `~/.irods/irods_environment.json`, set `IRODS_ENVIRONMENT_FILE` to load from a different location:

```
export IRODS_ENVIRONMENT_FILE=/full/path/to/different.json
```

Other individual environment variables can be set by using the UPPERCASE versions of the variables named above, for example:

```
export IRODS_LOG_LEVEL=7
```

3.4.5 CHECKSUM CONFIGURATION

Checksums in iRODS 4.0+ can be calculated using one of multiple hashing schemes. Since the default hashing scheme for iRODS 4.0+ is SHA256, some existing earlier checksums may need to be recalculated and stored in the iCAT.

The following two settings, the default hash scheme and the match hash policy, need to be set on both the client and the server.

Client (irods_environment.json)	Server (server_config.json)
irods_default_hash_scheme - SHA256 (default) - MD5	default_hash_scheme - SHA256 (default) - MD5
irods_match_hash_policy - Compatible (default) - Strict	match_hash_policy - Compatible (default) - Strict

When a request is made, the sender and receiver's hash schemes and the receiver's policy are considered:

Sender	Receiver	Result
MD5	MD5	Success with MD5
SHA256	SHA256	Success with SHA256
MD5	SHA256, Compatible	Success with MD5
MD5	SHA256, Strict	Error, USER_HASH_TYPE_MISMATCH
SHA256	MD5, Compatible	Success with SHA256
SHA256	MD5, Strict	Error, USER_HASH_TYPE_MISMATCH

If the sender and receiver have consistent hash schemes defined, everything will match.

If the sender and receiver have inconsistent hash schemes defined, and the receiver's policy is set to "compatible," the sender's hash scheme is used.

If the sender and receiver have inconsistent hash schemes defined, and the receiver's policy is set to "strict," a USER_HASH_TYPE_MISMATCH error occurs.

3.4.6   SPECIAL CHARACTERS

The default setting for "standard_conforming_strings" in PostgreSQL 9.1+ was changed to "on". Non-standard characters in iRODS Object names will require this setting to be changed to "off". Without the correct setting, this may generate a USER_INPUT_PATH_ERROR error.

3.5   PLUGIN INTERFACES

iRODS 4.0+ represents a major effort to analyze, harden, and package iRODS for sustainability, modularization, security, and testability. This has led to a fairly significant refactorization of much of the underlying codebase. The following descriptions are included to help explain the architecture of iRODS.

iRODS has been modularized whereby existing iRODS 3.x functionality has been replaced and provided by small, interoperable plugins.

The core is designed to be as immutable as possible and serve as a bus for handling the internal logic of the business of iRODS (data storage, policy enforcement, etc.). Seven major interfaces have been exposed by the core and allow extensibility and separation of functionality into plugins. A few plugins are included by default in iRODS to provide a set of base functionality.

The plugin interfaces are listed here:

Plugin Interface	Since
Pluggable Microservices	E-iRODS 3.0b2
Composable Resources	E-iRODS 3.0b3
Pluggable Authentication	E-iRODS 3.0.1b1
Pluggable Network	E-iRODS 3.0.1b1
Pluggable Database	iRODS 4.0.0b1
Pluggable RPC API	iRODS 4.0.0b2
Pluggable Rule Engine	iRODS 4.2.0

3.5.1   PLUGGABLE MICROSERVICES

One of the first plugin functionality to be completed was pluggable microservices. Pluggable microservices allow users to add new microservices to an existing iRODS server without recompiling the server or even restarting any running processes. A microservice plugin contains a single compiled microservice shared object file to be found and loaded by the server. Development examples can be found in Chapter 6.

A separate development package, irods-dev, contains the necessary header files to write your own microservice plugins (as well as any other type of iRODS plugin).

3.5.2   COMPOSABLE RESOURCES

The second type of plugins added to iRODS 4.0+ consists of composable resources. Composable resources replace the concept of resource groups from iRODS 3.x.

An iRODS composite resource is a tree with one "root" node. Nodes that are at the bottom of the tree are "leaf" nodes. Nodes that are not leaf nodes are "branch" nodes and have one or more "child" nodes. A child node can have one and only one "parent" node. To represent the functionality of a particular resources within a particular tree, the terms "coordinating" and "storage" are used in iRODS.

Coordinating resources coordinate the flow of data to and from other resources. A coordinating resource has built-in logic that defines how it determines, or coordinates, the flow of data to and from its children. Coordinating resources exist solely in the iCAT and exist virtually across all iRODS servers in a particular Zone. A storage resource has a Vault (physical) path and knows how to speak to a specific type of storage medium (disk, tape, etc.). The encapsulation of resources into a plugin architecture allows iRODS to have a consistent interface to all resources, whether they represent coordination or storage. Storage resources are typically "leaf" nodes and handle the direct reading and writing of data through a POSIX-like interface.

3.5.3   PLUGGABLE AUTHENTICATION

In iRODS 4.2, the authentication methods are contained in plugins. By default, similar to iRODS 3.3 and prior, iRODS comes with native iRODS challenge/response (password) enabled. However, enabling an additional authentication mechanism is as simple as adding a file to the proper directory. The server does not need to be restarted.

By default, iRODS uses a secure password system for user authentication. The user passwords are scrambled and stored in the iCAT database. Additionally, iRODS supports user authentication via PAM (Pluggable Authentication Modules), which can be configured to support many things, including the LDAP or Active Directory (AD) authentication systems. GSI and Kerberos are also available. PAM and SSL have been configured "available" out of the box with iRODS, but there is still some setup required to configure an installation to communicate with your external authentication server of choice.

3.5.4   PLUGGABLE NETWORK

iRODS now ships with both TCP and SSL network plugins enabled. The SSL mechanism is provided via OpenSSL and wraps the activity from the TCP plugin.

The SSL parameters are tunable via the following `irods_environment.json` variables:

```
"irods_client_server_negotiation": "request_server_negotiation",
"irods_client_server_policy": "CS_NEG_REQUIRE",
"irods_encryption_key_size": 32,
"irods_encryption_salt_size": 8,
"irods_encryption_num_hash_rounds": 16,
"irods_encryption_algorithm": "AES-256-CBC",
```

The only valid value for "irods_client_server_negotiation" at this time is "request_server_negotiation." Anything else will not begin the negotiation stage and default to using a TCP connection.

The possible values for "irods_client_server_policy" include the following.

- CS_NEG_REQUIRE: This side of the connection requires an SSL connection.

- CS_NEG_DONT_CARE: This side of the connection will connect either with or without SSL.

- CS_NEG_REFUSE: (default) This side of the connection refuses to connect via SSL.

On the server side, the `core.re` has a default value of "CS_NEG_DONT_CARE" in the acPreConnect() rule:

```
acPreConnect(*OUT) { *OUT="CS_NEG_DONT_CARE"; }
```

In order for a connection to be made, the client and server have to agree on the type of connection they will share. When both sides choose `CS_NEG_DONT_CARE`, iRODS shows an affinity for security by connecting via SSL. Additionally, it is important to note that all servers in an iRODS Zone are required to share the same SSL credentials (certificates, keys, etc.). Maintaining per-route certificates is not supported at this time.

The remaining parameters are standard SSL parameters and made available through the EVP library included with OpenSSL.

3.5.5 PLUGGABLE DATABASE

The iRODS metadata catalog is installed and managed by separate plugins. iRODS has PostgreSQL, MySQL, and Oracle database plugins available and tested.

The particular type of database is encoded in `/etc/irods/database_config.json` with the following directive:

```
"catalog_database_type" : "postgres",
```

This is populated by the `setup_irods.py` script on configuration.

The iRODS 3.x icatHighLevelRoutines are, in effect, the API calls for the database plugins. No changes should be needed to any calls to the icatHighLevelRoutines.

To implement a new database plugin, a developer will need to provide the existing 84 SQL calls (in icatHighLevelRoutines) and an implementation of GenQuery.

3.5.6 PLUGGABLE RPC API

The iRODS API has traditionally been a hard-coded table of values and names. With the pluggable RPC API now available, a plugin can provide new API calls.

At runtime, if a reqested API number is not already in the table, it is dynamically loaded from `plugins/api` and executed. As it is a dynamic system, there is the potential for collisions between existing API numbers and any new dynamically loaded API numbers. It is considered best practice to use a dynamic API number above 10,000 to ensure no collisions with the existing static API calls.

API plugins self-describe their IN and OUT packing instructions. These packing instructions are loaded into the table at runtime along with the API name, number, and the operation implementation being described.

All newly defined operations are architecturally assured of being wrapped in Dynamic Policy Enforcements Points (both a _pre and _post).

3.5.7   PLUGGABLE RULE ENGINE

iRODS 4.2+ introduced the iRODS rule engine plugin interface. This plugin interface allows iRODS administrators and users to write iRODS policy rules in languages other than the iRODS Rule Language.

Rule engine plugins are written in C++, installed on a particular iRODS server, and configured in that server's `server_config.json`.

The iRODS currently supports the following rule engine plugins:

- iRODS Rule Language Rule Engine Plugin

- Python Rule Engine Plugin

- C++ Default Policy Rule Engine Plugin

- C++ Audit (AMQP) Rule Engine Plugin

- JavaScript Rule Engine Plugin

The Rule Engine Plugin Framework (REPF), which keeps track of state and interprets both system-defined rules and user-defined rules, is a critical component of the iRODS system. Rules are definitions of actions that are to be performed by the server. These actions are defined in multiple ways, depending on the language that is used to define the actions. In the native iRODS Rule Language, the actions are defined with microservices and other actions. The REPF determines which defined rules are loaded and active and then delegates to the plugins to execute any relevant action. In the case of the iRODS Rule Language Rule Engine Plugin, it interprets the rules and calls the appropriate microservices. For the Python Rule Engine Plugin, it loads the python interpreter and executes the named function definitions as appropriate.

3.6   EXAMPLE PLUGINS

3.6.1   COMPOSABLE RESOURCES

Composable resources replace the concept of resource groups from iRODS 3.x. There are no resource groups in iRODS 4.0+.

Tree Metaphor

In computer science, a tree is a data structure with a hierarchical representation of linked nodes. These nodes can be named based on where they are in the hierarchy. The node at the top of a tree is the root node. Parent nodes and child nodes are on opposite ends of a connecting link, or edge. Leaf nodes are at the bottom of the tree, and any node that is not a leaf node is a branch node. These positional descriptors are helpful when describing the structure of a tree. Composable resources are best represented using this tree metaphor.

An iRODS composite resource is a tree with one "root" node. Nodes that are at the bottom of the tree are "leaf" nodes. Nodes that are not leaf nodes are "branch" nodes and have one or more "child" nodes. A child node can have one and only one "parent" node.

The terms root, leaf, branch, child, and parent represent locations and relationships within the structure of a particular tree. To represent the functionality of a particular resources within a particular tree, the terms "coordinating" and "storage" are used in iRODS. Coordinating resources coordinate the flow of data to and from other resources. Storage resources are typically "leaf" nodes and handle the direct reading and writing of data through a POSIX-like interface.

Any resource node can be a coordinating resource and/or a storage resource. However, for clarity and reuse, it is generally best practice to separate the two so that a particular resource node is either a coordinating resource or a storage resource.

This powerful tree metaphor is best illustrated with an actual example. You can now use `ilsresc` to visualize the tree structure of a Zone.

```
irods@hostname:~/ $ ilsresc
demoResc
randy:random
        pt1:passthru
                ufs5
        repl1:replication
                pt2:passthru
                        pt3:passthru
                                pt4:passthru
                ufs10
                ufs11
        ufs1
robin:roundrobin
        repl2:replication
                repl3:replication
                        ufs6
                        ufs7
                        ufs8
                ufs3
                ufs4
        ufs2
test
test1
test2
test3
```

Virtualization

In iRODS, files are stored as Data Objects on disk and have an associated physical path as well as a virtual path within the iRODS file system. iRODS collections, however, only exist in the iCAT database and do not have an associated physical path (allowing them to exist across all resources, virtually).

Composable resources, both coordinating and storage, introduce the same dichotomy between the virtual and physical. A coordinating resource has built-in logic that defines how it determines, or coordinates, the flow of data to and from its children. Coordinating resources exist solely in the iCAT and exist virtually across all iRODS servers in a particular Zone. A storage resource has a Vault (physical) path and knows how to speak to a specific type of storage medium (disk, tape, etc.). The encapsulation of resources into a plugin architecture allows iRODS to have a consistent interface to all resources, whether they represent coordination or storage.

This virtualization enables the coordinating resources to manage both the placement and the retrieval of Data Objects independent from the types of resources that are connected as children resources. When iRODS tries to retrieve data, each child resource will "vote," indicating whether it can provide the requested data. Coordinating resources will then decide which particular storage resource (e.g., physical location) the read should come from. The specific manner of this vote is specific to the logic of the coordinating resource. A coordinating resource may lean toward a particular vote based on the type of optimization it deems best. For instance, a coordinating resource could decide between child votes by opting for the child that will reduce the number of requests made against each storage resource within a particular time frame or opting for the child that reduces latency in expected data retrieval times. We expect a wide variety of useful optimizations to be developed by the community.

An intended side effect of the tree metaphor and the virtualization of coordinating resources is the deprecation of the concept of a resource group. Resource groups in iRODS 3.x could not be put into other resource groups. A specific limiting example is a compound resource that, by definition, was a group and could not be placed into another group. This significantly limited its functionality as a management tool. Groups in iRODS now only refer to user groups.

Coordinating Resources

Coordinating resources contain the flow control logic which determines both how its child resources will be allocated copies of data as well as which copy is returned when a Data Object is requested. There are several types of coordinating resources: compound, random, replication, round robin, passthru, and some additional types that are expected in the future. Each is discussed in more detail below.

Compound   The compound resource is a continuation of the legacy compound resource type from iRODS 3.x.

A compound resource has two and only two children. One must be designated as the "cache" resource and the other as the "archive" resource. This designation is made in the "context string" of the addchildtoresc command.

An Example:

```
irods@hostname:~/ $ iadmin addchildtoresc parentResc
    ↪ newChildResc1 cache
irods@hostname:~/ $ iadmin addchildtoresc parentResc
    ↪ newChildResc2 archive
```

Putting files into the compound resource will first create a replica on the cache resource and then create a second replica on the archive resource.

This compound resource auto-replication policy can be controlled with the context string associated with a compound resource. The key "auto_repl" can have the value "on" (default), or "off".

For example, to turn off the automatic replication when creating a new compound resource (note the empty host/path parameter):

```
irods@hostname:~/ $ iadmin mkresc compResc compound '' auto_repl=
    ↪ off
```

When auto-replication is turned off, it may be necessary to replicate on demand. For this scenario, there is a microservice named msisync_to_archive() which will sync (replicate) a data object from the child cache to the child archive of a compound resource. This creates a new replica within iRODS of the synchronized data object.

Getting files from the compound resource will behave in a similar way as iRODS 3.x. By default, the replica from the cache resource will always be returned. If the cache resource does not have a copy, then a replica is created on the cache resource before being returned.

This compound resource staging policy can be controlled with the policy key-value pair whose keyword is "compound_resource_cache_refresh_policy" and whose values are either "when_necessary" (default), or "always."

From the example near the bottom of the core.re rulebase:

```
# =-=-=-=-=-=-
# policy controlling when a dataObject is staged to cache from
    ↪ archive in a compound coordinating resource
# - the default is to stage when cache is not present ("
    ↪ when_necessary")
# =-=-=-=-=-=-
# pep_resource_resolve_hierarchy_pre( *OUT ){*OUT="
    ↪ compound_resource_cache_refresh_policy=when_necessary";}  #
    ↪  default
```

```
# pep_resource_resolve_hierarchy_pre( *OUT ){*OUT="
    ↪ compound_resource_cache_refresh_policy=always";}
```

Replicas within a compound resource can be trimmed. There is no rebalance activity defined for a compound resource. When the cache fills up, the administrator will need to take action as they see fit. This may include physically moving files to other resources, commissioning new storage, or marking certain resources "down" in the iCAT.

The --purgec option for iput, iget, and irepl is honored and will always purge the first replica (usually with replica number 0) for that Data Object (regardless of whether it is held within this compound resource). This is not an optimal use of the compound resource as the behavior will become somewhat nondeterministic with complex resource compositions.

Deferred   The deferred resource is designed to be as simple as possible. A deferred resource can have one or more children.

A deferred resource provides no implicit data management policy. It defers to its children with respect to routing both puts and gets. However they vote, the deferred node decides.

Load Balanced   The load-balanced resource provides equivalent functionality as the "doLoad" option for the msiSetRescSortScheme microservice. This resource plugin will query the r_server_load_digest table from the iCAT and select the appropriate child resource based on the load values returned from the table.

The r_server_load_digest table is part of the Resource Monitoring System and has been incorporated into iRODS 4.x. The r_server_load_digest table must be populated with load data for this plugin to function properly.

The load-balanced resource has an effect on writes only (it has no effect on reads).

Random   The random resource provides logic to put a file onto one of its children on a random basis. A random resource can have one or more children.

If the selected target child resource of a put operation is currently marked "down" in the iCAT, the random resource will move on to another random child and try again. The random resource will try each of its children, and if still not succeeding, throw an error.

Replication   The replication resource provides logic to automatically manage replicas to all its children.

Rebalancing of the replication node is made available via the "rebalance" subcommand of iadmin. For the replication resource, all Data Objects on all children will be replicated to all other children. The amount of work done in each iteration as the looping mechanism completes is controlled with the session variable replication_rebalance_limit. The default value is set at 500 Data Objects per loop.

Getting files from the replication resource will show a preference for locality. If the client is connected to one of the child resource servers, then that replica of the file will be returned, minimizing network traffic.

Round Robin   The round robin resource provides logic to put a file onto one of its children on a rotating basis. A round robin resource can have one or more children.

If the selected target child resource of a put operation is currently marked "down" in the iCAT, the round robin resource will move onto the next child and try again. If all the children are down, then the round robin resource will throw an error.

Passthru   The passthru resource was originally designed as a testing mechanism to exercise the new composable resource hierarchies. They have proven to be more useful than that in a couple of interesting ways.

1. A passthru can be used as the root node of a resource hierarchy. This will allow a Zone's users to have a stable default resource, even as an administrator changes out disks or other resource names in the Zone.

2. A passthru resource's contextString can be set to have an effect on its child's votes for both read and/or write.

To create a resource with priority read, use a "read" weight greater than 1 (note the empty host:path parameter):

```
irods@hostname:~/ $ iadmin mkresc newResc passthru '' 'write=1.0;
    ↪ read=2.0'
Creating resource:
Name:           "newResc"
Type:           "passthru"
Host:           ""
Path:           ""
Context:        "write=1.0;read=2.0"
```

To modify an existing passthru resource to be written to only after other eligible resources, use a "write" weight less than 1:

```
irods@hostname:~/ $ iadmin modresc newResc context 'write=0.4;
    ↪ read=1.0'
```

A passthru resource can have one and only one child.

Nondeterministic behavior will occur if a passthru resource is configured with more than one child. The plugin will take action on whichever child is returned by the catalog.

Storage Resources

Storage resources represent storage interfaces and include the file driver information to talk with different types of storage.

UnixFileSystem   The unixfilesystem storage resource is the default resource type that can communicate with a device through the standard POSIX interface.

A high water mark capability has been added to the unixfilesystem resource in 4.1.8. The high water mark can be configured with the context string using the following syntax:

```
irods@hostname:~/ $ iadmin modresc unixResc context '
    ↪ high_water_mark=1000'
```

The value is the total disk space used in bytes. If a create operation would result in the total bytes on disk being larger than the high water mark, then the resource will return USER_FILE_TOO_LARGE and the create operation will not occur. This feature allows administrators to protect their systems from absolute disk full events. Writing to, or extending, existing file objects is still allowed.

A free_space check capability has been added to the unixfilesystem resource in 4.1.10. The free_space check can be configured with the context string using the following syntax:

```
irods@hostname:~/ $ iadmin modresc unixResc context '
    ↪ minimum_free_space_for_create_in_bytes=21474836480'
```

The example requires this unixfilesystem plugin instance (unixResc) to keep 20 GiB free when considering whether to accept a create operation. If a create operation would result in the bytes free on disk being smaller than the set value, then the resource will return USER_FILE_TOO_LARGE and the create operation will not occur. This feature allows administrators to protect their systems from absolute disk full events. Writing to, or extending, existing file objects is still allowed and not affected by this setting.

The check that is performed by the unixfilesystem plugin instance compares the minimum_free_space_for_create_in_bytes value from the context string to the free_space value stored in the R_RESC_MAIN (resource) table in the iCAT. The free_space ↪ value in the catalog can be updated with iadmin modresc freespace or with the msi_update_unixfilesystem_resource_free_space(*leaf_resource) on every server where unixfilesystems are active.

To update the free_space value from the command line (manually) to 1 TiB, the following iadmin command can be used:

```
irods@hostname:~/ $ iadmin modresc unixResc freespace
    ↪ 1099511627776
```

To update the free_space value after every large file put and replication (automatically), the following rules can be used:

```
acPostProcForParallelTransferReceived(*leaf_resource) {
    msi_update_unixfilesystem_resource_free_space(*leaf_resource)
        ↪ ;
}
```

```
acPostProcForDataCopyReceived(*leaf_resource) {
    msi_update_unixfilesystem_resource_free_space(*leaf_resource)
        ↪ ;
}
```

acPostProcForParallelTransferReceived is only triggered by parallel transfer, so puts of small files will not cause iRODS to update the free_space entry of a resource. However, when the small file is replicated (by, e.g., a replication resource) the free_space of the resource receiving the replica will be updated, because acPostProcForDataCopyReceived is hit by both large and small files.

To use a blacklist of resources (that you do not want updated), that can be implemented directly in the rule logic:

```
acPostProcForParallelTransferReceived(*leaf_resource) {
    *black_list = list("some", "of", "the", "resources");
    *update_free_space = 1;
    foreach(*resource in *black_list) {
        if (*resource == *leaf_resource) {
            *update_free_space = 0;
            break;
        }
    }
    if (*update_free_space) {
        msi_update_unixfilesystem_resource_free_space(*
            ↪ leaf_resource);
    }
}
acPostProcForDataCopyReceived(*leaf_resource) {
    *black_list = list("some", "of", "the", "resources");
    *update_free_space = 1;
    foreach(*resource in *black_list) {
        if (*resource == *leaf_resource) {
            *update_free_space = 0;
            break;
        }
    }
    if (*update_free_space) {
        msi_update_unixfilesystem_resource_free_space(*
            ↪ leaf_resource);
    }
}
```

Structured File Type (tar, zip, gzip, bzip)   The structured file type storage resource is used to interface with files that have a known format. By default these are used "under the covers" and are not expected to be used directly by users (or administrators).

These are used mainly for mounted collections.

Amazon S3 (Archive)   The Amazon S3 archive storage resource is used to interface with an S3 bucket. It is expected to be used as the archive child of a compound resource composition. The credentials are stored in a file which is referenced by the context string.

DDN WOS (Archive)   The DataDirect Networks (DDN) WOS archive storage resource is used to interface with a Web Object Scalar (WOS) Appliance. It is expected to be used as the archive child of a compound resource composition. It currently references a single WOS endpoint and WOS policy in the context string.

HPSS   The HPSS storage resource is used to interface with an HPSS storage management system. It can be used as the archive child of a compound resource composition or as a first class resource in iRODS. The connection information is referenced in the context string.

Non-Blocking   The non-blocking storage resource behaves exactly like the standard unix file system storage resource except that the "read" and "write" operations do not block (they return immediately while the read and write happen independently).

Mock Archive   The mock archive storage resource was created mainly for testing purposes to emulate the behavior of object stores (e.g., WOS). It creates a hash of the file path as the physical name of the Data Object.

Universal Mass Storage Service   The univMSS storage resource delegates `stage_to_cache` and `sync_to_arch` operations to an external script which is located in the `msiExecCmd_bin` directory. It currently writes to the Vault path of that resource instance, treating it as a unix file system.

When creating a "univmss" resource, the context string provides the location of the Universal MSS script.

Example:

```
irods@hostname:~/ $ iadmin mkresc myArchiveResc univmss HOSTNAME
    ↪ :/full/path/to/Vault univMSSInterface.sh
```

Managing Child Resources

There are two new `iadmin` subcommands introduced with this feature.

addchildtoresc:

```
addchildtoresc Parent Child [ContextString] (add child to
    ↪ resource)
```

Add a child resource to a parent resource. This creates an "edge" between two nodes in a resource tree. Parent is the name of the parent resource. Child is the name of the child resource. ContextString is any relevant information that the parent may need in order to manage the child.
>   rmchildfromresc:

```
rmchildfromresc Parent Child (remove child from resource)
```

Remove a child resource from a parent resource. This removes an "edge" between two nodes in a resource tree. Parent is the name of the parent resource. Child is the name of the child resource.

Example Usage

Creating a composite resource consists of creating the individual nodes of the desired tree structure and then connecting the parent and children nodes. Example: Replicates Data Objects to three locations.

A replicating coordinating resource with three unix file system storage resources as children would be composed with seven (7) `iadmin` commands:

```
irods@hostname:~/ $ iadmin mkresc example1 replication
irods@hostname:~/ $ iadmin mkresc repl_resc1 unixfilesystem renci
    ↪ .example.org:/Vault
irods@hostname:~/ $ iadmin mkresc repl_resc2 unixfilesystem
    ↪ sanger.example.org:/Vault
irods@hostname:~/ $ iadmin mkresc repl_resc3 unixfilesystem eudat
    ↪ .example.org:/Vault
irods@hostname:~/ $ iadmin addchildtoresc example1 repl_resc1
irods@hostname:~/ $ iadmin addchildtoresc example1 repl_resc2
irods@hostname:~/ $ iadmin addchildtoresc example1 repl_resc3
```

Rebalancing

A new subcommand for `iadmin` allows an administrator to rebalance a coordinating resource. The coordinating resource can be the root of a tree, or anywhere in the middle of a tree. The `rebalance` operation will rebalance for all decendents. For example, the `iadmin` command `iadmin modresc` ↪ `myReplResc rebalance` would fire the rebalance operation for the replication resource instance named `myReplResc`. Any Data Objects on `myReplResc` that did not exist on all its children would be replicated as expected.

For other coordinating resource types, rebalance can be defined as appropriate. For coordinating resources with no concept of "balanced," the rebalance operation is a "no op" and performs no work.

3.6.2   PLUGGABLE AUTHENTICATION

In iRODS 4.2, the authentication methods are contained in plugins. iRODS comes with native iRODS challenge/response (password) enabled. Enabling an additional authentication mechanism is as simple as adding a file to the proper directory. By default, iRODS uses a secure password system for user authentication. The user passwords are scrambled and stored in the iCAT database. Additionally, iRODS supports user authentication via PAM (Pluggable Authentication Modules).

The iRODS administrator can "force" a particular authentication scheme for a rodsuser by "blanking" the native password for the rodsuser. There is currently no way to signal to a particular login attempt that it is using an incorrect scheme.

GSI (Grid Security Infrastructure)

Grid Security Infrastructure (GSI) setup in iRODS 4.0+ has been greatly simplified.

GSI Configuration   Configuration of GSI is out of scope for this document, but consists of the following three main steps.

1. Install GSI (most easily done via package manager).

2. Confirm the (default) irods service account has a certificate in good standing (signed).

3. Confirm the local system account for client "newuser" has a certificate in good standing (signed).

iRODS Configuration   Configuring iRODS to authenticate via GSI requires a few simple steps.
First, if GSI is being configured for a new user, it must be created:

```
iadmin mkuser newuser rodsuser
```

Then that user must be configured so its Distiguished Name (DN) matches its certificate:

```
iadmin aua newuser '/DC=org/DC=example/O=Example/OU=People/CN=New
    ↪   User/CN=UID:drexample'
```

!!! Note: The comma characters (,) in the Distiguished Name (DN) must be replaced with forward slash characters (/).

On the client side, the user's "irods_authentication_scheme" must be set to "GSI." This can be configured via an `irods_environment.json` property:

```
"irods_authentication_scheme": "GSI",
```

Then, to authenticate with a temporary proxy certificate:

```
grid-proxy-init
```

This will prompt for the user's GSI password. If the user is successfully authenticated, temporary certificates are issued and setup in the user's environment. The certificates are good, by default, for 24 hours.

In addition, if users want to authenticate the server, they can set "irods_gsi_server_dn" in their user environment. This will cause the system to do mutual authentication instead of just authenticating the client user to the server.

Limitations The iRODS administrator will see two limitations when using GSI authentication.

1. The "client_user_name" environment variable will fail (the admin cannot alias as another user).

2. The `iadmin moduser password` will fail (cannot update the user's password).

    The workaround is to use iRODS native authentication when using these.

`ipasswd` for rodsusers will also fail, but it is not an issue as it would be trying to update their (unused) iRODS native password. They should not be updating their GSI passwords via iCommands.

Kerberos

Kerberos setup in iRODS 4.0+ has been greatly simplified. The functionality itself is provided by the Kerberos authentication plugin.

Kerberos Configuration Configuration of a Kerberos server for authentication is out of scope for this document, but consists of the following four main steps.

1. Set up Kerberos (Key Distribution Center (KDC) and Kerberos Admin Server).

2. Confirm the (default) irods service account has a service principal in KDC (with the hostname of the rodsServer) (e.g., irodsserver/serverhost.example.org@EXAMPLE.ORG).

3. Confirm the local system account for client "newuser" has principal in KDC (e.g., newuser@EXAMPLE.ORG).

4. Create an appropriate keytab entry (adding to an existing file or creating a new one).

    A new keytab file can be created with the following command:

```
kadmin ktadd -k /var/lib/irods/irods.keytab irodsserver/
    ↪ serverhost.example.org@EXAMPLE.ORG
```

iRODS Configuration Configuring iRODS to authenticate via Kerberos requires a few simple steps.

First, if Kerberos is being configured for a new user, the new user must be created:

```
iadmin mkuser newuser rodsuser
```

Then that user must be configured so its principal matches the KDC:

```
iadmin aua newuser newuser@EXAMPLE.ORG
```

The /etc/irods/server_config.json must be updated to include:

```
"KerberosServicePrincipal": "irodsserver/serverhost.example.
    ↪ org@EXAMPLE.ORG",
"KerberosKeytab": "/var/lib/irods/irods.keytab",
```

An /etc/irods/server_config.json environment variable must also be included to point the GSS API to the keytab mentioned above:

```
"environment_variables": {
    "KRB5_KTNAME": "/var/lib/irods/irods.keytab"
},
```

On the client side, the user's "irods_authentication_scheme" must be set to "KRB." This can be configured via an irods_environment.json property:

```
"irods_authentication_scheme": "KRB",
```

Then, to initialize the Kerberos session ticket and authenticate:

```
kinit
```

Limitations   The iRODS administrator will see two limitations when using Kerberos authentication.

1. The "clientUserName" environment variable will fail (the admin cannot alias as another user).

2. The `iadmin moduser password` will fail (cannot update the user's password).

The workaround is to use iRODS native authentication when using these.

ipasswd for rodsusers will also fail, but it is not an issue as it would be trying to update their (unused) iRODS native password. They should not be updating their Kerberos passwords via iCommands.

Weak Encryption Workaround   If you are seeing either of the errors GSS-API error ↪ initializing context: KDC has no support for encryption type   or KRB_ERROR_INIT_SECURITY_CONTEXT when setting up Kerberos, then you probably have an available cypher mismatch between the Kerberos server and the Active Directory (AD) server. This is not an iRODS setting, and can be addressed in the Kerberos configuration.

The MIT Key Distribution Center (KDC) uses the most secure encoding type when sending the ticket to the AD server. When the AD server is unable to handle that encoding, it replies with the error that the encryption type is not supported.

To override this mismatch and allow a weaker algorithm to be sufficient, set `allow_weak_crypto = yes` in the `libdefaults` stanza of `/etc/krb5.conf`:

```
$ head /etc/krb5.conf
[libdefaults]
        default_realm = EXAMPLE.ORG
        allow_weak_crypto = yes
...
```

This will allow the Kerberos handshake to succeed, which allows the iRODS connection to continue.

PAM (Pluggable Authentication Module)

User Setup PAM can be configured to to support various authentication systems; however the iRODS administrator still needs to add the users to the iRODS database:

```
irods@hostname:~/ $ iadmin mkuser newuser rodsuser
```

If the user's credentials will be exclusively authenticated with PAM, a password need not be assigned.

For PAM Authentication, the iRODS user selects the new iRODS PAM authentication choice (instead of Native, or Kerberos) via an `irods_environment.json` property:

```
"irods_authentication_scheme": "PAM",
```

Then, the user runs "iinit" and enters their system password. To protect the system password, SSL (via OpenSSL) is used to encrypt the `iinit` session.

Configuring the operating system, the service name used for PAM is "irods." An addition to /etc/pam.d/ is required if the fall-through behavior is not desired.

For example: ~ $ cat /etc/pam.d/irods auth required pam_env.so auth sufficient pam_unix.so auth requisite pam_succeed_if.so uid >= 500 quiet auth required pam_deny.so ~

A quick test for the basic authentication mechanism for PAM is to run the `iRODS/server` ↪ `/bin/PamAuthCheck` tool. PamAuthCheck reads the password from stdin (without any prompting).

If PamAuthCheck returns `Not Authenticated`, that suggests that PAM is not set up correctly. You will need to configure PAM correctly (and therefore get PamAuthCheck returning Authenticated) before using PAM through iRODS.

A simple way to check that you are using PamAuthCheck correctly, and that it is the PAM settings that need updated, is to create a fully permissive PAM setup with the following command.

```
sudo su - root -c 'echo "auth sufficient pam_permit.so" > /etc/
    ↪ pam.d/irods'
```

This will allow any username/password combination to successfully authenticate with the irods PAM service, meaning that any username/password combination should cause PamAuthCheck to return `Authenticated`.

With the permissive configuration working with PamAuthCheck, the next step is to adjust your PAM configuration to your desired settings (LDAP, in this case). You will know that is correct when PamAuthCheck behaves as you would expect when using LDAP username/passwords. iRODS uses PamAuthCheck directly, so if it is working on the command line, it should work when run by iRODS.

Since PAM requires the user's password in plaintext, iRODS relies on SSL encryption to protect these credentials. PAM authentication makes use of SSL regardless of the iRODS Zone SSL configuration (meaning even if iRODS explicitly does *not* encrypt data traffic, PAM will use SSL during authentication).

In order to use the iRODS PAM support, you also need to have SSL working between the iRODS client and server. The SSL communication between client and iRODS server needs some basic setup in order to function properly. Much of the setup concerns getting a proper X.509 certificate setup on the server side, and setting up the trust for the server certificate on the client side. You can use either a self-signed certificate (best for testing) or a certificate from a trusted CA.

Server Configuration   The following keywords are used to set values for PAM server configuration. These were previously defined as compile-time options. They are now configurable via the `/etc/irods/server_config.json` configuration file. The default values have been preserved.

- pam_password_length

- pam_no_extend

- pam_password_min_time

- pam_password_max_time

Server SSL Setup   Here are the basic steps to configure the server:

- **Generate a new RSA key.** Make sure it does not have a passphrase (i.e., do not use the -des, -des3 or -idea options to genrsa):

  ```
  irods@hostname:~/ $ openssl genrsa -out server.key
  ```

- **Acquire a certificate for the server.** The certificate can be either from a trusted CA (internal or external), or can be self-signed (common for development and testing). To request a certificate from a CA, create your certificate signing request, and then follow the instructions given by the CA. When running the "openssl req" command, some questions will be asked about what to put in the certificate. The locality fields do not really matter from the point of view of verification, but you probably want to try to be accurate. What is important, especially since this is a certificate for a server host, is to make sure to use the FQDN of the server as the "common name" for the certificate (should be the same name that clients use as their irods_host), and do not add an email address. If you are working with a CA, you can also put host aliases that users might use to access the host in the "subjectAltName" X.509 extension field if the CA offers this capability.

To generate a Certificate Signing Request that can be sent to a CA, run the "openssl req" command using the previously generated key:

```
irods@hostname:~/ $ openssl req -new -key server.key -out
    ↪ server.csr
```

To generate a self-signed certificate, also run "openssl req," but with slightly different parameters. In the openssl command, you can put as many days as you wish:

```
irods@hostname:~/ $ openssl req -new -x509 -key server.key -
    ↪ out server.crt -days 365
```

- **Create the certificate chain file.** If you are using a self-signed certificate, the chain file is just the same as the file with the certificate (server.crt). If you have received a certificate from a CA, this file contains all the certificates that together can be used to verify the certificate, from the host certificate through the chain of intermediate CAs to the ultimate root CA.

An example best illustrates how to create this file. A certificate for a host "irods.example.org" is requested from the proper domain registrar. Three files are received from the CA: irods.crt, PositiveSSLCA2.crt and AddTrustExternalCARoot.crt. The certificates have the following "subjects" and "issuers":

```
openssl x509 -noout -subject -issuer -in irods.crt
subject= /OU=Domain Control Validated/OU=PositiveSSL/CN=irods
    ↪ .example.org
issuer= /C=GB/ST=Greater Manchester/L=Salford/O=COMODO CA
    ↪ Limited/CN=PositiveSSL CA 2
openssl x509 -noout -subject -issuer -in PositiveSSLCA2.crt
subject= /C=GB/ST=Greater Manchester/L=Salford/O=COMODO CA
    ↪ Limited/CN=PositiveSSL CA 2
issuer= /C=SE/O=AddTrust AB/OU=AddTrust External TTP Network/
    ↪ CN=AddTrust External CA Root
openssl x509 -noout -subject -issuer -in
    ↪ AddTrustExternalCARoot.crt
```

```
subject= /C=SE/O=AddTrust AB/OU=AddTrust External TTP Network
    ↪ /CN=AddTrust External CA Root
issuer= /C=SE/O=AddTrust AB/OU=AddTrust External TTP Network/
    ↪ CN=AddTrust External CA Root
```

The irods.example.org cert was signed by the PositiveSSL CA 2, and that the PositiveSSL CA 2 cert was signed by the AddTrust External CA Root, and that the AddTrust External CA Root cert was self-signed, indicating that it is the root CA (and the end of the chain).

To create the chain file for irods.example.org:

```
irods@hostname:~/ $ cat irods.crt PositiveSSLCA2.crt
    ↪ AddTrustExternalCARoot.crt > chain.pem
```

- **Generate OpenSSL parameters.** Generate some Diffie-Hellman parameters for OpenSSL:

```
irods@hostname:~/ $ openssl dhparam -2 -out dhparams.pem 2048
```

- **Place files within accessible area.** Put the dhparams.pem, server.key and chain.pem files somewhere that the iRODS server can access them (e.g., in /etc/irods). Make sure that the irods unix user can read the files (although you also want to make sure that the key file is only readable by the irods user).

- **Set the iRODS SSL environment.** The server expects to have the following irods service account's irods_environment.json properties set on startup:

```
"irods_ssl_certificate_chain_file": "/etc/irods/chain.pem",
"irods_ssl_certificate_key_file": "/etc/irods/server.key",
"irods_ssl_dh_params_file": "/etc/irods/dhparams.pem",
```

- **Restart iRODS.** Restart the server:

```
irods@hostname:~/ $ ./iRODS/irodsctl restart
```

Client SSL Setup   The client may or may not require configuration at the SSL level, but there are a few parameters that can be set via irods_environment.json properties to customize the client SSL interaction if necessary. In many cases, if the server's certificate comes from a common CA, your system might already be configured to accept certificates from that CA, and you will not have to adjust the client configuration at all. For example, on an Ubuntu12 (Precise) system, the /etc/ssl/certs directory is used as a repository for system trusted certificates installed via an Ubuntu package. Many of the commercial certificate vendors such as VeriSign and AddTrust have their certificates already installed.

After setting up SSL on the server side, test SSL by using the PAM authentication (which requires an SSL connection) and running iinit with the log level set to LOG_NOTICE. If you see messages as follows, you need to set up trust for the server's certificate, or you need to turn off server verification.

Error from non-trusted self-signed certificate:

```
irods@hostname:~/ $ IRODS_LOG_LEVEL=LOG_NOTICE iinit
NOTICE: environment variable set, irods_log_level(input)=
    ↪ LOG_NOTICE, value=5
NOTICE: created irods_home=/dn/home/irods
NOTICE: created irods_cwd=/dn/home/irods
Enter your current PAM (system) password:
NOTICE: sslVerifyCallback: problem with certificate at depth: 0
NOTICE: sslVerifyCallback:    issuer = /C=US/ST=North Carolina/L=
    ↪ Chapel Hill/O=RENCI/CN=irods.example.org
NOTICE: sslVerifyCallback:    subject = /C=US/ST=North Carolina/L=
    ↪ Chapel Hill/O=RENCI/CN=irods.example.org
NOTICE: sslVerifyCallback:    err 18:self signed certificate
ERROR: sslStart: error in SSL_connect.
SSL error: error:14090086:SSL routines:
    ↪ SSL3_GET_SERVER_CERTIFICATE:certificate verify failed
sslStart failed with error -2103000 SSL_HANDSHAKE_ERROR
```

Error from untrusted CA that signed the server certificate:

```
irods@hostname:~/ $ IRODS_LOG_LEVEL=LOG_NOTICE iinit
NOTICE: environment variable set, irods_log_level(input)=
    ↪ LOG_NOTICE, value=5
NOTICE: created irods_home=/dn/home/irods
NOTICE: created irods_cwd=/dn/home/irods
Enter your current PAM (system) password:
NOTICE: sslVerifyCallback: problem with certificate at depth: 1
NOTICE: sslVerifyCallback:    issuer = /C=US/ST=North Carolina/O=
    ↪ example.org/CN=irods.example.org Certificate Authority
NOTICE: sslVerifyCallback:    subject = /C=US/ST=North Carolina/O=
    ↪ example.org/CN=irods.example.org Certificate Authority
NOTICE: sslVerifyCallback:    err 19:self signed certificate in
    ↪ certificate chain
ERROR: sslStart: error in SSL_connect.
SSL error: error:14090086:SSL routines:
    ↪ SSL3_GET_SERVER_CERTIFICATE:certificate verify failed
sslStart failed with error -2103000 SSL_HANDSHAKE_ERROR
```

Server verification can be turned off using the irods_ssl_verify_server `irods_environment` ↪ `.json` property. If this variable is set to "none," then any certificate (or none) is accepted by the client. This means that your connection will be encrypted, but you cannot be sure to what server (i.e., there is no server authentication). For that reason, this mode is discouraged.

It is much better to set up trust for the server's certificate, even if it is a self-signed certificate. The easiest way is to use the irods_ssl_ca_certificate_file `irods_environment.json` property to contain all the certificates of either hosts or CAs that you trust. If you configured the server as described above, you could just set the following property in your `irods_environment.json`:

```
"irods_ssl_ca_certificate_file": "/etc/irods/chain.pem"
```

Or this file could just contain the root CA certificate for a CA-signed server certificate. Another potential issue is that the server certificate does not contain the proper FQDN (in either the Common Name field or the subjectAltName field) to match the client's "irods_host" property. If this situation cannot be corrected on the server side, the client can set:

```
"irods_ssl_verify_server": "cert"
```

Then, the client library will only require certificate validation, but will not check that the hostname of the iRODS server matches the hostname(s) embedded within the certificate.

Encryption Settings The following SSL encryption settings are required in `irods_environment.json` on both sides of the connection (client and server) and the values must match.

- `irods_encryption_algorithm` (required) — EVP-supplied encryption algorithm for parallel transfer encryption.

- `irods_encryption_key_size` (required) — Key size for parallel transfer encryption.

- `irods_encryption_num_hash_rounds` (required) — Number of hash rounds for parallel transfer encryption.

- `irods_encryption_salt_size` (required) — Salt size for parallel transfer encryption.

Environment Variables All the `irods_environment.json` properties used by the SSL support (both server and client side) are listed below.

irods_ssl_certificate_chain_file (server) The file containing the server's certificate chain. The certificates must be in PEM format and must be sorted starting with the subject's certificate (actual client or server certificate), followed by intermediate CA certificates if applicable, and ending at the highest level (root) CA.

irods_ssl_certificate_key_file (server) Private key corresponding to the server's certificate in the certificate chain file.

irods_ssl_dh_params_file (server) The Diffie-Hellman parameter file location.

irods_ssl_verify_server (client) What level of server certificate based authentication to perform. "none" means not to perform any authentication at all. "cert" means to verify the certificate validity (i.e., that it was signed by a trusted CA). "hostname" means to validate the certificate and to verify that the `irods_host`'s FQDN matches either the common name or one of the subjectAltNames of the certificate. "hostname" is the default setting.

irods_ssl_ca_certificate_file (client) Location of a file of trusted CA certificates in PEM format. Note that the certificates in this file are used in conjunction with the system default trusted certificates.

irods_ssl_ca_certificate_path (client) Location of a directory containing CA certificates in PEM format. The files each contain one CA certificate. The files are looked up by the CA subject name hash value, which must be available. If more than one CA certificate with the same name hash value exist, the extension must be different (e.g., 9d66eef0.0, 9d66eef0.1, etc.). The search is performed based on the ordering of the extension number, regardless of other properties of the certificates. Use the `c_rehash` utility to create the necessary links.

CHAPTER 4

Rule-Oriented Programming

ROP is a different (although not new) paradigm from normal programming practice. In ROP, the power of controlling the functionality rests more with the users than with system and application developers. Hence, any change to a particular process or policy can be easily constructed by the user, and then tested and deployed without the aid of system and application developers.

ROP can be viewed as lego-block type programming. The building blocks for the ROP are "microservices." Microservices are small, well-defined procedures/functions that perform a specific task. Microservices are developed and made available by system programmers and application programmers. Users and administrators can "chain" these microservices to implement a larger macro-level functionality that they want to use or provide for others. For example, one of the microservices might be to "createCollection," another one might be to "computeChecksum," and a third to "replicateObject."

Larger macro-level functionalities are called Actions. Since one can perform an Action in more than one way, each Action might have one or more chains of microservices associated with it. Hence, one can view an Action as the name of a task, and the chains of microservices as the procedural counterpart for performing the task. Since there may be more than one chain of microservices possible for an Action, iRODS provides two mechanisms for finding the best choice of microservice to apply in a given situation. The first mechanism is a "condition" that can be attached to any microservice chain, which will be tested for compliance before executing the chain. These conditions, in effect, act as guards that check for permission for execution of the chain. The triplet "action, condition, chain" is called a "Rule" in the ROP system.

The second mechanism that is used for identifying an applicable Rule is a "priority" associated with a chain. In the current implementation, the priority is associated with the order in which the Rules are read from Rule files upon initialization.

The earlier the Rule is read and included in the Rule Base, the higher its priority compared to all the Rules for the same Action.

The implementation of iRODS includes another helpful feature. The chain of microservices is not limited to only microservice procedures and functions, but can also include Actions. Hence, when executing a chain of microservices, if an Action needs to be performed the system will invoke the Rule application program for the new Action. Thus, an Action can be built using other Actions. Care should be taken so that there are no infinite cycles in any loop formed by recursive calls to the same Action.

In summary, the first three components of a Rule consist of an action name, a testable condition, and a chained workflow consisting of actions and microservices. The order of the Rule in the Rule Base determines its priority.

The fourth component of a Rule is a set of recovery microservices. An important question that arises is, what should be done when a microservice fails (returns a failure). A microservice failure means that the chain has failed and hence that the instance of the Action has failed. But as mentioned above, there can be more than one way to perform an Action. Therefore, when a failure is encountered, one can try to execute another Rule of a lower priority for that Action. When doing this, a decision must be made about the changes that were made to variables generated by the failing chain of microservices. In particular, any side effects (such as a physical file creation on a disk) that might have happened as a result of successful microservice execution before the failure must be handled. The same question applies to any changes made to the metadata stored in the iCAT.

The iRODS architecture is designed so that if one Rule for an Action fails, another applicable Rule of lower priority is attempted. If one of these Rules succeeds, then the Action is considered successful. To make sure that the failing chain of microservices does not leave any changes and side effects, we provide the following mechanism. For every microservice in the chain in a Rule, the Rule designer specifies a "recovery microservice or Action" that is listed in the same order as in the chain.

A recovery microservice is just like any microservice, but with the functionality that it recovers from the task rather than performs a task. A recovery microservice should be able to recover from the multiple types of errors that can result from an execution of the corresponding microservice. More importantly, a recovery microservice should also be able to recover from a successful microservice execution. This feature is needed because in the chain of microservices, when a downstream microservice fails, one needs to recover from all changes and side effects performed, not only those of the specific failing microservice but also those of all the successful microservices in the chain performed before the failed microservice. The recovery mechanism for an Action is of the same type as that of a recovery microservice, although one only needs to recover from successful completion of a Rule, when a later microservice/Rule fails in the chain. If an Action fails, by definition, any Rule for that Action would have recovered from the effects of the failed Action.

During the recovery process, the recovery microservices for all the successful microservices will be performed, so that when completed, the effect of the Rule for that Action is completely neutralized. Hence, when an alternate, lower priority Rule is tried for the same Action, it starts with the same initial setting used by the failed Rule. This property of complete recovery from failure is called the "atomicity" property of a Rule. Either a Rule is fully successful with attendant changes and side effects completed, or the state is unchanged from the time of invocation. If all Rules for a particular Action fail, one can see that the system is left in the same state as if the Rule was not executed. One can view this as a "transactional" feature for Actions. The concepts of atomicity and transactions are adopted from relational databases.

In summary, every Rule has an Action name, a testable condition, a chain of Actions and microservices, and a corresponding chain of recovery Actions and microservices. Each Rule also has an associated priority.

For example, consider a very simple Rule for data ingestion into iRODS, with two microservices, "createPhysicalFile" and "registerObject," and no conditions. The Rule creates a copy of the file in an iRODS storage vault and registers the existence of the file into the iCAT Metadata Catalog. The Data Grid administrator can define an alternate Rule of a higher priority, which can also check whether the data type of the file is "DICOM image file" and invoke an additional microservice called "extractDICOMMetadata" to populate the iCAT with metadata extracted from the file, after the file has been created on the iRODS Server and registered in the iCAT Metadata Catalog.

We did not implement the idea that an Action or microservice should be implicitly tied to a single recovery Action or microservice. Although this might make it easier to find a recovery service by this implicit link, we recognized that recovery from an Action or microservice can be dependent on where and how it is being invoked. Sometimes, a simpler recovery would do the trick instead of a more complex recovery. For instance, a database rollback might suffice if one knew that the Action started a new iCAT Metadata Catalog database transaction. Otherwise, a longer sequence of recovery delete/insert and update SQL statements is needed to recover from multiple SQL statement activities. So, we give the Rule designer the ability to tie in the appropriate recovery for each microservice or Action as part of the Rule instead of having the system or application designer who develops the microservice do this.

The iRODS Rule Language Rules are stored in "iRODS Rule Base" files (with extension ".re"). These files are located in the /etc/irods/ directory. One can specify use of more than one .re file that will be read one after the other during initialization. The set of .re files to be used is decided by the iRODS administrator by setting values in the /etc/irods/server_config.json file. The administrator can include more than one Rule Base file. The files are read in the order they are given in the configuration file and the Rules are prioritized in the order they are read. By default, the Rule Base to be used is the `core.re` file.

Now that we have seen what comprises a Rule, an Action, and a microservice, we will next look at how a Rule is invoked and what type of mechanisms are available to communicate with the microservices and Actions. As one can see, microservices (by this, we also mean Actions) do not operate in a vacuum. They need input and produce output and communicate with other microservices, make changes to the iCAT database, and have side effects such as file creation. Hence, the question arises, what information do the Rules operate on?

To answer this question, we need the concept of a *session*. A session is a single iRODS Server invocation. The session starts when a client connects to the iRODS Server and ends when the Client disconnects. During the session, there are two distinct "state information" spaces that are operated upon by Actions and microservices.

- **Persistent State Information** is defined by the attributes and schema that are stored in the iCAT catalog.

- **Session State Information** is temporary information that is maintained in the memory as a C-struct only during the period when the Actions are being performed.

The Persistent State Information is the content that is available across sessions and persists in the iCAT Metadata Catalog after the Action has been performed, provided proper commit operations were performed before the end of the session. The Session State Information does not persist between sessions but is a mechanism for microservices to communicate with each other during the session without going to the database to retrieve every attribute value. One can view the Persistent State Information as a "persistent blackboard" through which sessions communicate with each other (sessions possibly started by different users). Similarly, one can view Session State Information as a "temporary blackboard" that manages within a session some of the state information needed by Actions and microservices. Note that Session State Information persists beyond a single Action, and hence when one is performing multiple Actions during a single session, the memory of the earlier Actions (unless destroyed or overwritten) can be utilized by a current Action.

The Session State Information structure is a complex C structure, called the Rule Execution Infrastructure (REI). To hide the physical nature of the Session State Information structure, we adopt a Logical Name Space that can support extensions to the physical structure. The Session State Information Logical Name Space defines a set of "$variables" that map to a value node in the REI structure. This mapping is defined by "data variable mapping" files (files with extensions ".dvm"), which are located in the /etc/irods directory. The $variable mapping defines how the system can translate a $variable name to a path name in the REI structure. For persons implementing microservices, iRODS provides "C" functions that allow users to obtain the runtime address of the denoted value. One can have more than one definition for a $variable name. This is needed because different microservices might use the same $variables to denote different paths in the REI structure. The function for obtaining values from the REI structure will cycle through these definitions to get to the first non-NULL value. We strongly recommend the use of unique definitions for each $variable, and we advocate that designers use multiple definitions only under very controlled circumstances.

The Persistent State Information Variables have a Logical Name Space defined by the attribute set of the iCAT Metadata Catalog. The mappings from Persistent State Variables to columns in tables in the iCAT schema are defined in lib/core/include/rodsGenQuery.h. These variables can be queried using the generic query call `iquest` available for accessing data from the iCAT database. The command

```
iquest attrs
```

lists the persistent state information attributes.

4.1 SESSION STATE VARIABLES

The $variables can be used as input to a Rule, can also be used to define input to a microservice, and can be used to define output from a microservice that will be used by subsequent microservices. The addition of new variables to the Data Grid requires the recompilation of the software. Thus, an attempt has been made to provide a complete set of variables needed for the management and access of files within a Data Grid. In practice, only a small fraction of these variables is needed for most administrator-modified Rules.

Not all Session Variables are available for every action performed in iRODS. Only those Session Variables that are pertinent to a specific action are automatically set. The availability of each Session Variable for Rules listed in the core.re file depends on the nature of the operation when the Rule is invoked. For example, when the iRODS Server is performing operations on a data object when the Rule is invoked, data object type Session Variables will generally be available for the microservices referenced by the Rule.

In Section 5.3, the correlation between available Session Variables and the Rules in the default core.re file is listed. The Session Variables that are automatically available when interactively executing a Rule are also defined.

4.2 PERSISTENT STATE INFORMATION VARIABLES

The system Persistent State Information that is generated by application of microservices is stored in the iCAT Metadata Catalog. The iCAT catalog can be queried. The source file

```
lib/core/include/rodsGenQuery.h
```

defines the columns available via the General Query interface. Each of the names for a column (metadata attribute or item of state information) begins with COL_ (column) for easy identification throughout the source code. The iquest client program also uses these field names but without the COL_ prefix.

The Persistent State Information variables are based on a Logical Name Space as defined by the attribute set of the iCAT Metadata Catalog. These variables can be queried using the generic query call iquest, which is available for accessing data from the iCAT database. Executing the command iquest attrs will list all of the Persistent State Information Variables.

CHAPTER 5

The iRODS Rule System

iRODS rules can generally be classified into two Rule Classes.

1. **System-level rules**. These are rules invoked on the iRODS Servers internally to enforce/execute Management Policies for the system. Examples of policies include data management policies such as enforcement of authenticity, integrity, access restrictions, data placement, data presentation, replication, distribution, pre- and post-processing, and metadata extraction and assignment. Other examples are the automation of services such as administration, authentication, authorization, auditing, and accounting. Within the iRODS framework, policy enforcement points have been explicitly defined. Whenever an enforcement point is reached, iRODS invokes the associated policy, which is read from the core.re file.

2. **User-level rules**. The iRODS Rule Engine can also be invoked externally by clients through the irule command or the `rcExecMyRule` API. Typically, these are workflow-type rules that allow users to request that the iRODS Servers perform a sequence of operations (microservices) on behalf of the user. In addition to providing useful services to users, this type of operation can be very efficient because the operations are done on the servers where the data are located.

Some rules require immediate execution, whereas others may be executed at a later time in the background (depending on the Rule Execution mode). The *Delayed Execution Service* allows rules/microservices to be queued and executed at a later time by the Rule Execution Server. Examples of microservices that are suitable for delayed execution are post-processing operations such as checksuming, replication, and metadata extraction. For example, the post-processing microservice msiExtractNaraMetadata was specifically designed to extract and register metadata from National Archives and Records Administration (NARA) Archival Information Locator data objects (NAIL files) that have been uploaded into a NARA collection.

rules that have been written into a file can be executed through the `irule` command:

```
irule---vF Rulename.r
```

The `irule` command has the following input parameters as listed by the help package:

```
Usage: irule [--available]
Usage: irule [--test] [-v] [-r instanceName] rule inputParam
    ↪ outParamDesc
Usage: irule [--test] [-v] [-l] [-r instanceName] -F inputFile [
    ↪ prompt | arg_1 arg_2 ...]
```

The `irule` command submits a user defined rule to be executed by an iRODS server.

The format of the rules follows the specification given in Section 5.6. The input can be specified through the command line or can be read from the .r file using the −F option.

The first form above list all available rule engine instances.

The second form above requires three inputs:

1. rule—This is the rule to be executed.

2. inputParam—The input parameters. The input values for the rule is specified here. If there is no input, a string containing "null" must be specified.

3. outParamDesc—Description for the set of output parameters to be returned. If there is no output, a string containing "null" must be specified.

The third form above reads the rule and arguments from the file: inputFile. The file containing the rule must have three parts.

1. The first line specifies the rule. The iRODS Rule Language supports multiple rules in the .r file when it is used as input to the `irule` command. The first rule will be evaluated and all the rules included in the .r will be available during the execution of the first rule before the `irule` command returns.

2. The second line specifies the input arguments as `label=value` pairs separated by % '

    • If % is needed in an input value, use %%.

    • An input value can begin with $. In such a case the user will be prompted. A default value can be listed after the $, as in *A=$40. If prompted, the default value will be used if the user presses return without giving a replacement.

    • The input line can just be the word `null`.

3. The third line contains output parameters as labels separated by %.

    • The built-in variable `ruleExecOut` stores output from the rule generated by microservices.

    • The output line can just be the word `null`.

arg_1 is of the form *arg=value. For example, using *A=$ as one of the arguments in line 2 of the `inputFile`, `irule` will prompt for *A or the user can enter it on the command line:

```
irule -F filename *A=23
```

or

```
irule -F filename "*A='/path/of/interest'" *B=24
irule -F filename "*A=\"/path/of/interest\"" *B=24
```

Your shell may require escaping and/or single quotes.

The options on the `irule` command are:

- `--string,-s` enable string mode, in string mode all command line input arguments do not need to be quoted and are automatically converted to strings string mode does not affect input parameter values in rule files

- `--file,-F inputFile` read the file for the input if the inputFile begins with the prefix "i:" then the file is fetched from an iRODS server

- `--list,-l` list file if -F option is used

- `--verbose,-v` verbose

- `--available,-a` list all available rule engine instances

- `--rule-engine-plugin-instance,-r` specify a particular other instance of rule engine plugin to run rule on

- `--help,-h` this help

If an input parameters is preceded by the symbol \$, the `irule` command prompts for a new value for the attribute value.

With the addition of rule engine plugins, `irule` now has a way to specify which rule engine should be running any submitted code snippet.

By default, `irule` will submit its code snippet (or named rulefile) to the rule engine plugin listed first in the `rule_engines` array of `server_config.json`.

To specify a particular other instance of rule engine plugin, `irule` must use the -r flag:

```
$ irule -r irods_rule_engine_plugin-irods_rule_language-instance
    ↪ -F myrulefile.r
```

5.1 THE IRODS RULE ARCHITECTURE

At the core of the iRODS Rule System is the iRODS Pluggable Rule Engine System, which runs on all iRODS Servers. A Rule Engine can invoke a number of predefined microservices based on the interpretation of the rule being executed.

The underlying operations that need to be performed are based on C functions that operate on internal C structures. The external view of the execution architecture is based on Actions (typically called tasks) that need to be performed, and external input parameters (called Attributes) that are used to guide and perform these Actions. The C functions themselves are abstracted externally by giving them logical names (we call the functions "internal microservices" and the abstractions "external microservices"). To make the links between the external world and the internal C apparatus transparent, we define mappings from client libraries to rules. Moreover, since the operations that are performed by iRODS need to change the Persistent State Information in the ICAT Metadata Catalog, the attributes are mapped to the persistent Logical Name Space for metadata names that are used in the ICAT.

The foundation for the iRODS architecture is based on the following key concepts, partially discussed in Chapter 4 on ROP.

1. A Persistent Database that shares data (facts) across time and users.

2. A Transient Memory that holds data during a session.

3. A set of Actions (T) that name and define the tasks that need to be performed.

4. A set of internal, well-defined, callable microservices (P) made up of procedures and functions that provide the methods for executing the subtasks that need to be performed.

5. A set of external Attributes (A) that is used as a Logical Name Space to externally refer to data and metadata.

6. A set of external microservices (M) (or methods) that is used as a Logical Name Space to externally refer to functions that are chained together within a rule.

7. A set of rules (R) that defines what needs to be done for each Action (T) and is based on A and M.

5.2   DEFAULT iRODS RULES

The `core.re` file contains the rules that are applied by default when an iRODS Data Grid is created. These rules are typically modified by the Data Grid Administrator to impose the data Management Policies for the shared collection. For example, the modifications can be specific to a data collection, or to a data type, or to a storage resource, or to a user group.

These rules can be thought of as policy hooks into the operation of the iRODS Data Grid that enable different policies to be enforced at the discretion of the Data Grid Administrator. There are 72 places where policy can be enforced, typically at the start of a request to create or modify data, collections, users, or resources; or after the end of a request to create or modify data, collections, users, or resources.

Multiple versions of each rule can be placed in the `core.re` file. The rule listed closest to the top of the core.re file will be executed first. If the rule does not meet the required condition or fails, the next version of the rule will be tried. A generic version of the rule should be included that will apply if all of the higher priority rules fail. Note that most of the rules in the default core.re file are placeholders that do not execute any microservices. The `core.re` file contains multiple examples of each rule that have been commented out by inserting a # symbol at the beginning of the line.

The purpose for each rule is listed. They can be loosely organized into rules related to users, resources, collections, data manipulation, metadata manipulation, and rule application. Most of the data and metadata manipulation policies can be applied either before an operation within the iRODS framework is executed or after the operation is completed. Typical policies applied before the operation include authorization, resource selection, approval flags, and conversion of input parameters. Typical policies applied after an operation is completed include format transformation, delayed replication, integrity checks, and data subsetting.

5.3   SESSION VARIABLES AVAILABLE FOR DEFAULT iRODS RULES

When a policy enforcement point is reached within the iRODS framework, associated Session Variables will be available. The Session Variables may be used within a rule to decide between options and control the execution of the rule. Not all Session Variables are available at each policy enforcement point. In particular, note that a limited set of Session Variables are available when rules are executed interactively.

The available Session Variables can be grouped into seven sets: (1) *SuserAndConn*, (2) *SdataObj1*, (3) *SdataObj2*, (4) *SrescInfo*, (5) *Scollection*, (6) *SuserAdmin1*, and (7) *SuserAdmin2*.

1. The *SuserAndConn* (S1) set contains Session Variables relating to information about the client user and the current client/server connection. This set includes userName-Client, rodsZoneClient, privClient, authStrClient, userAuthSchemeClient, userName-Proxy, rodsZoneProxy, privProxy, authStrProxy, userAuthSchemeProxy, otherUser, connectCnt, connectSock, connectOption, connectStatus, and connectApiTnx. This set of Session Variables should be available in all rules.

2. The *SdataObj1* (S2) set contains just one Session Variable, objPath. It is available in pre-processing rules before a data object is created.

3. The *SdataObj2* (S3) set contains Session Variables relating to information on a data object. This set includes objPath, dataType, dataSize, chksum, version, filePath, replNum, replStatus, writeFlag, dataOwner, dataOwnerZone, dataComments, dataAccess, dataAccessInx, dataId, collId, statusString, destRescName, and backupRescName.

4. The *SrescInfo* (S4) set contains Session Variables relating to information on an iRODS data storage resource. This set includes rescName, rescGroupName, zoneName, rescLoc, rescType, rescTypeInx, rescClass, rescClassInx, rescVaultPath, rescMaxObjSize, freeSpace, freeSpaceTimeStamp, rescInfo, rescId, and rescComments.

5. The *Scollection* (S5) set contains Session Variables relating to information on a Collection. This set includes collName and collParentName.

6. The *SuserAdmin1* (S6) set contains Session Variables relating to information on users for administration purposes. This set includes otherUserName, otherUserZone, and otherUserType.

7. The *SuserAdmin2* (S7) set contains Session Variables for information on new users. This set includes otherUserName and otherUserZone.

The available variable sets for some of the default rules are as follows:

acSetRescSchemeForCreate	SdataObj1 and SuserAndConn
acPreprocForDataObjOpen	SdataObj2 and SrescInfo and SuserAndConn
acSetMultiReplPerResc	SuserAndConn
acPostProcForPut	SdataObj2 and SrescInfo and SuserAndConn
acPostProcForCopy	SdataObj2 and SrescInfo and SuserAndConn
acPostProcForFilePathReg	SdataObj2 and SrescInfo and SuserAndConn
acPostProcForCreate	SdataObj2 and SrescInfo and SuserAndConn
acPostProcForOpen	SdataObj2 and SrescInfo and SuserAndConn
acSetNumThreads	SuserAndConn
acDataDeletePolicy	SdataObj2 and SrescInfo and SuserAndConn
acPostProcForDelete	SdataObj2 and SrescInfo and SuserAndConn
acNoChkFilePathPerm	SdataObj2 and SrescInfo and SuserAndConn
acTrashPolicy	SdataObj1 and SuserAndConn
acSetPublicUserPolicy	SuserAndConn
acSetPublicUserPolicy	SuserAndConn
acSetVaultPathPolicy	SdataObj2 and SrescInfo and SuserAndConn
acSetReServerNumProc	SuserAndConn
acPreprocForCollCreate	Scollection and SuserAndConn
acPostProcForCollCreate	Scollection and SuserAndConn
acPretProcForRmColl	Scollection and SuserAndConn
acPostProcForRmColl	Scollection and SuserAndConn
acPreProcForModifyUser	SuserAndConn
acPostProcForModifyUser	SuserAndConn
acPreProcForModifyAVUmetadata	SuserAndConn
acPostProcForModifyAVUmetadata	SuserAndConn
acPreProcForCreateUser	SuserAndConn
acPostProcForCreateUser	SuserAndConn
acPreProcForDeleteUser	SuserAndConn
acPostProcForDeleteUser	SuserAndConn
acPreProcForCreateResource	SuserAndConn
acPostProcForCreateResource	SuserAndConn
acPreProcForCreateToken	SuserAndConn

acPostProcForCreateToken	SuserAndConn
acPreProcForModifyUserGroup	SuserAndConn
acPostProcForModifyUserGroup	SuserAndConn
acPreProcForDeleteResource	SuserAndConn
acPostProcForDeleteResource	SuserAndConn
acPreProcForDeleteToken	SuserAndConn
acPostProcForDeleteToken	SuserAndConn
acPreProcForModifyResource	SuserAndConn
acPostProcForModifyResource	SuserAndConn
acPreProcForModifyCollMeta	Scollection and SuserAndConn
acPostProcForModifyCollMeta	Scollection and SuserAndConn
acPreProcForModifyDataObjMeta	SdataObj1 and SuserAndConn
acPostProcForModifyDataObjMeta	SdataObj1 and SuserAndConn
acPreProcForModifyAccessControl	SuserAndConn
acPostProcForModifyAccessControl	SuserAndConn
acPreProcForObjRename	SdataObj1 and SuserAndConn
acPostProcForObjRename	SdataObj1 and SuserAndConn
acPreProcForGenQuery	SuserAndConn
acPostProcForGenQuery	SuserAndConn
acCreateUser	SuserAdmin and SuserAndConn
acCreateUserF1	SuserAdmin1 and SuserAndConn
acCreateDefaultCollections	SuserAdmin1 and SuserAndConn
acCreateUserZoneCollections	SuserAdmin1 and SuserAndConn
acCreateCollByAdmin	SuserAndConn
acDeleteUser	SuserAdmin2 and SuserAndConn
acDeleteUserF1	SuserAdmin2 and SuserAndConn
acDeleteDefaultCollections	SuserAdmin2 and SuserAndConn
acDeleteUserZoneCollections	SuserAndConn
acDeleteCollByAdmin	SuserAndConn
acRenameLocalZone	SuserAndConn
acGetUserByDN	SuserAndConn
acAclPolicy	None

When microservices are executed using the `irule` command, only the S1 set will be available for the referenced microservices.

5.4   DYNAMIC POLICY ENFORCEMENT POINTS

iRODS 4.0+ has introduced the capability for dynamic policy enforcement points (PEP). For every operation that is called, two policy enforcement points are constructed (both a pre and post variety), and if it has been defined in core.re or any other loaded rulebase file they will be executed by the rule engine plugin framework.

The PEP will be constructed of the form pep_PLUGINOPERATION_pre and pep_ ↪ PLUGINOPERATION_post.

For example, for `resource_create`, the two PEPs that are dynamically evaluated are `pep_resource_create_pre` and `pep_resource_create_post`. If either or both have been defined in a loaded rulebase file (`core.re`), they will be executed as appropriate. If the same PEP is multiply defined, the first one loaded will be executed first. If the first one fails, the next matching PEP will execute until there are no more matches in the loaded rulebases. This matching is carried out by the rule engine plugin framework and will match across multiple active rule engine plugins.

5.4.1   FLOW CONTROL

The flow of information from the pre PEP to the plugin operation to the post PEP works as follows:

`pep_PLUGINOPERATION_pre` Should produce an *OUT variable that will be passed to the calling plugin operation. PLUGINOPERATION will receive any OUT defined by `pep_PLUGINOPERATION_pre` above and will pass its own OUT variable to pep_ ↪ PLUGINOPERATION_post

`pep_PLUGINOPERATION_post()` will receive any OUT from PLUGINOPERATION. If the PLUGINOPERATION itself failed, the OUT variable will be populated with the string "OPERATION_FAILED".

Note that if `pep_PLUGINOPERATION_pre` fails, the PLUGINOPERATION will not be called and the plugin operation call will fail with the resulting error code of the pep_ ↪ PLUGINOPERATION_pre rule call. This ability to fail early allows for fine-grained control of which plugin operations may or may not be allowed as defined by the policy of the data grid administrator.

5.4.2   PARAMETER SERIALIZATION

The rule engine plugin framework serializes many of the parameters at the plugin operation point of call. This provides the maximum amount of information for the administrator to make policy decisions within a particular policy enforcement point (PEP).

Many of these internal types within iRODS have been provided serialization functions. Those that have not will be passed as an empty variable into each dynamic PEP. Users can reference the types provided for each dynamic PEP with the following table which contains the types that have been serialized.

```
float*
const std::string*
std::string*
```

```
std::string
hierarchy_parser*
rodsLong_t
rodsLong_t*
size_t
int
int*
char*
const char*
rsComm_t*
plugin_context
dataObjInp_t*
authResponseInp_t*
dataObjInfo_t*
keyValPair_t*
userInfo_t*
collInfo_t*
modAVUMetadataInp_t*
modAccessControlInp_t*
modDataObjMeta_t*
ruleExecSubmitInp_t*
dataObjCopyInp_t*
rodsObjStat_t**
rodsObjStat_t*
genQueryInp_t*
genQueryInp_t*
char**
```

5.4.3 DYNAMIC PEP SIGNATURES

Within the iRODS Rule Language the signatures for dynamic PEPs are determined by the invocation of the plugin operation within the iRODS Agent.

Since this is a dynamic process, the following example demonstrates how to implement a chosen dynamic PEP. For all operations that are not part of the API interface, the context is wrapped by the instance name and the out variable. Any additional parameters must be included in the signature of the dynamic PEP (the rule name).

For example:

```
pep_resource_resolve_hierarchy_pre(
  irods::plugin_context & _ctx,
```

```
const std::string * _opr,
const std::string * _curr_host,
irods::hierarchy_parser * _out_parser,
float * _out_vote)
```

should be implemented as:

```
pep_resource_resolve_hierarchy_pre(*INSTANCE_NAME, *CONTEXT, *OUT
   ↪ , *OPERATION, *HOST, *PARSER, *VOTE){}
```

Note the following direct substitutions:

(injected)	*INSTANCE_NAME
irods::plugin_context & _ctx	*CONTEXT
(injected)	*OUT
const std::string * _opr	*OPERATION
const std::string * _curr_host	*HOST
irods::hierarchy_parser * _out_parser	*PARSER
float * _out_vote	*VOTE

*INSTANCE_NAME and *OUT are automatically injected by the rule engine plugin framework. The dynamic PEPs for API operations do not include *CONTEXT, and *OUT:

```
pep_api_data_obj_put_pre(rsComm_t * rsComm,
                         dataObjInp_t * dataObjInp,
                         bytesBuf_t * dataObjInpBBuf,
                         portalOprOut_t ** portalOprOut)
```

becomes:

```
pep_api_data_obj_put_pre(*INSTANCE_NAME, *COMM, *DATAOBJINP, *
   ↪ BUFFER, *PORTAL_OPR_OUT)
```

After *INSTANCE_NAME, note the next two types of this signature are serialized by the framework, but the last two are not. This means that the information within *COMM and *
↪ DATAOBJINP will be available in the rule logic whereas *BUFFER and *PORTAL_OPR_OUT will explain they are not supported.

An example of the five variables and their resolved values are shown here:

*INSTANCE_NAME	api_instance
*COMM	auth_scheme=native++++client_addr=X.X.X.X++++...
*DATAOBJINP	create_mode=0++++dataIncluded=++++dataType=generic++++...
*BUFFER	[BytesBuf*] not supported
*PORTAL_OPR_OUT	[portalOprOut**] not supported

Any PEP signature mismatches will appear in the rodsLog.

5.5   PLUGGABLE RULE ENGINE ARCHITECTURE

iRODS 4.2+ introduced the iRODS rule engine plugin interface. This plugin interface allows iRODS administrators and users to write iRODS policy rules in languages other than the iRODS Rule Language.

Rule engine plugins are written in C++, installed on a particular iRODS server, and configured in that server's `server_config.json`. iRODS currently supports the following rule engine plugins:

- iRODS Rule Language Rule Engine Plugin;

- Python Rule Engine Plugin;

- C++ Default Policy Rule Engine Plugin;

- C++ Audit (AMQP) Rule Engine Plugin; and

- JavaScript Rule Engine Plugin.

5.5.1   RULE ENGINE PLUGIN FRAMEWORK

The Rule Engine Plugin Framework (REPF), which keeps track of state and interprets both system-defined rules and user-defined rules, is a critical component of the iRODS system. Rules are definitions of actions that are to be performed by the server. These actions are defined in multiple ways, depending on the language that is used to define the actions. In the native iRODS Rule Language, the actions are defined with microservices and other actions. The REPF determines which defined rules are loaded and active and then delegates to the plugins to execute any relevant action. In the case of the iRODS Rule Language Rule Engine Plugin, it interprets the rules and calls the appropriate microservices. For the Python Rule Engine Plugin, it loads the python interpreter and executes the named function definitions as appropriate.

5.5.2   CONFIGURATION (server_config.json)

Because the rule engine plugins are just one of many iRODS plugin types, the REPF is configured within the following stanza in `server_config.json`:

```
{
    "plugin_configuration": {
        "rule_engines": []
    }
}
```

Within the rule engine plugin framework, there is a dynamically created policy enforcement point that is checked before and after every operation. These are the "_pre" and "_post" PEPs discussed in Section 5.4.

An example configuration is shown as follows:

```
{
    "plugin_configuration": {
        "rule_engines": [
            {
                "instance_name": "irods_rule_engine_plugin-python
                    ↪ -instance",
                "plugin_name": "irods_rule_engine_plugin-python",
                "plugin_specific_configuration": {}
            }
            {
                "instance_name": "irods_rule_engine_plugin-
                    ↪ irods_rule_language-instance",
                "plugin_name": "irods_rule_engine_plugin-
                    ↪ irods_rule_language",
                "plugin_specific_configuration": {
                    "re_data_variable_mapping_set": [
                        "core"
                    ],
                    "re_function_name_mapping_set": [
                        "core"
                    ],
                    "re_rulebase_set": [
                        "example",
                        "core"
                    ],
                    "regexes_for_supported_peps": [
                        "ac[^ ]*",
                        "msi[^ ]*",
                        "[^ ]*pep_[^ ]*_(pre|post)"
                    ]
                },
                "shared_memory_instance": "
                    ↪ irods_rule_language_rule_engine"
            }
        ]
    }
}
```

The framework will look for rules that are defined with the same name as the PEP and execute them if found. A typical `ils` will trigger over 1,200 dynamic PEPs on a basic installation. Nearly all of them will be undefined (there is no rule that matches their name) and so will not run any code.

However, any that *do* match a particular PEP will be executed in the order in which they are loaded. If there is only one matching rule, then it will fire and its return code will be interpreted by the REPF. If it fails, then the operation fails as well and an error is returned to the client (or to the log when run by the delay execution server.)

5.6   THE iRODS RULE LANGUAGE

The iRODS Rule Language is a domain specific language (DSL) provided by iRODS to define policies and actions in the system. The iRODS Rule Language is tightly integrated with other components of iRODS. Many frequently used policies and actions can be configured easily by writing simple rules, yet the language is flexible enough to allow complex policies or actions to be defined.

Everything is a rule in the iRODS Rule Language. A typical rule looks like:

```
acPostProcForPut {
  on($objPath like "*.txt") {
    msiDataObjCopy($objPath,"$objPath.copy");
  }
}
```

In this rule, the rule name `acPostProcForPut` is an event hook defined in iRODS. iRODS automatically applies this rule when certain events are triggered. The `on(...)` clause is a rule condition. The `{...}` block following the rule condition is a sequence of actions that is executed if the rule condition is true when the rule is applied. And the customary hello world rule looks like:

```
HelloWorld {
  writeLine("stdout", "Hello, world!");
}
```

In the following sections, we go over some features of the rule engine.

5.6.1   COMMENTS

The rule engine parses characters between the # token and the end of line as comments. Therefore, a comment does not have to occupy its own line. For example,

```
*A=1; # comments
```

Although the parser is able to parse comments starting with `##`, it is not recommended to start comments with `##`, as `##` is also used in the one line rule syntax as the actions connector. It is recommended to start comments with `#`.

5.6.2   DIRECTIVES

Directives are used to provide the rule engine with compile time intructions. The `@include` directive allows including a different rule base file into the current rule base file, similar to `#include` in C. For example, if we have a rule base file "definitions.re," then we can include it with the following directive `@include "definitions"`.

5.6.3   BOOLEAN AND NUMERIC

Boolean Literals
Boolean literals include `true` and `false`.

Boolean Operators
Boolean operators include

```
!  # not
&& # and
|| # or
%% # or used in the ## syntax
```

For example:

```
true && true
false && true
true || false
false || false
true %% false
false %% false
! true
```

Numeric Literals
Numeric literals include integral literals and double literals. An integral literal does not have a decimal while a double literal does. For example,

```
1 # integer
1.0 # double
```

In the iRODS Rule Language, an integer can be converted to a double. The reverse is not always true. A double can be converted to an integer only if the fractional part is zero. The rule engine provides two functions that can be used to truncate the fractional part of a double: `floor()` and `ceiling()`.

Integers and doubles can be converted to booleans using the `bool()` function. `bool()` converts 1 to `true` and 0 to `false`.

Arithmetic Operators

Arithmetic operators include, ordered by precedence:

```
-   # Negation
^   # Power
*   # Multiplication
/   # Division
%   # Modulo
-   # Subtraction
+   # Addition
>   # Greater than
<   # Less than
>= # Greater than or equal
<= # Less than or equal
```

Arithmetic Functions

Arithmetic functions include:

```
exp(<num>)
log(<num>)
abs(<num>)
floor(<num>)
ceiling(<num>)
average(<num>,<num>,...)
max(<num>,<num>,...)
min(<num>,<num>,...)
```

For example:

```
exp(10)
log(10)
abs(-10)
floor(1.2)
ceiling(1.2)
average(1,2,3)
max(1,2,3)
min(1,2,3)
```

5.6.4 STRINGS

String Literals

The rule engine requires by default that every string literal is quoted. The quotes can be either matching single quotes `'This is a string.'` or double quotes `"This is a string."`

If a programmer needs to quote strings containing single (double) quotes using single (double) quotes, then the quotes in the strings should be escaped using a backslash `"\"`, just as in the C Programming Language. For example,

```
writeLine("stdout", "\"\"");
# output ""
```

Single quotes inside double quotes are viewed as regular characters, and vice versa. They can be either escaped or not escaped. For example,

```
writeLine("stdout", "'");
# output '
```

```
writeLine("stdout", "\'");
# output '
```

The rule engine also supports various escaped characters:

```
\n, \r, \t, \', \", \$, \*
```

An asterisk should always be escaped if it is a regular character and is followed by letters.

Converting Values of Other Types to Strings

The `str()` function converts a value of type BOOLEAN, INTEGER, DOUBLE, DATE-TIME, or STRING to string. For example

```
writeLine("stdout", str(123));
# output 123
```

In addition,

```
timestrf(*time, *format)
```

converts a datetime stored in `*time` to a string, according to the `*format` parameter.

```
timestr(*time)
```

converts a datetime stored in `*time` to a string, according to the default format of `%b  %d  %Y  %H`
↪ `:%M:%S`. An example would be `Jun  01  2015  16:12:13`.

The format string uses the same directives as the standard C library.

Converting Strings to Values of Other Types

String can be converted to values of type BOOLEAN, INTEGER, DOUBLE, DATETIME, or STRING. For example

```
int("123")
double("123")
bool("true")
```

In addition,

```
datetimef(*str, *format)
```

converts a string stored in *str to a datetime, according to the *format parameter

```
datetime(*str)
```

converts a string stored in *str to a datetime, according to the default format (%b %d %Y %H:% ↪ M:%S, e.g., Jun 01 2015 16:12:13). It can also be used to convert an integer or a double to a datetime.

The following are examples of string datetime conversion:

```
datetime(*str)
datetimef(*str, "%Y␣%m␣%d␣%H:%M:%S")
timestr(*time)
timestrf(*time, "%Y␣%m␣%d␣%H:%M:%S")
```

String Functions

The rule engine supports the infix string concatenation operator "++"

```
writeLine("stdout", "This␣"++"␣is␣"++"␣a␣string.");
# output This is a string.
```

Infix wildcard expression matching operator: like

```
writeLine("stdout", "This␣is␣a␣string." like "This␣is*");
# Output: true
```

Infix regular expression matching operator: like regex

```
writeLine("stdout", "This␣is␣a␣string." like regex "This.*string
    ↪ [.]");
# Output: true
```

Substring: substr()

```
writeLine("stdout", substr("This␣is␣a␣string.", 5, 9));
# or
```

```
writeLine("stdout", substr("This␣is␣a␣string.", 5, 5+4));
# Output: is a
```

Length: strlen()

```
writeLine("stdout", strlen("This␣is␣a␣string."));
# Output: 17
```

Split: split()

```
writeLine("stdout", split("This␣is␣a␣string.", "␣"));
# Output: [This,is,a,string.]
```

Trim left: triml(*str, *del), which trims from *str the leftmost *del, inclusive.

```
writeLine("stdout", triml("This␣is␣a␣string.", "i"));
# Output: s is a string.
```

Trim right: trimr(*str, *del), which trims from *str the rightmost *del, inclusive.

```
writeLine("stdout", trimr("This␣is␣a␣string.", "r"));
# Output: This is a st
```

Variable Expansion

In a quoted string, an asterisk followed immediately by a variable name (without whitespaces) makes an expansion of the variable. For example,

```
"This␣is␣*x."
```

is equivalent to

```
"This␣is␣"++str(*x)++"."
```

Rules for Quoting Action Arguments

A parameter to a microservice is of type string if the expected type is MS_STR_T or STRING. When a microservice expects a parameter of type string and the argument is a string constant, the argument has to be quoted. For example,

```
writeLine("stdout", "This␣is␣a␣string.");
```

When a microservice expects a parameter of type string and the argument is not of type string, a type error may be thrown. For example,

```
*x = 123;
strlen(*x);
```

This error can be fixed by either using the "str" function

```
strlen(str(*x));
```

or putting *x into quotes

```
strlen("*x");
```

Action names and keywords such as for, while, assign are not arguments. Therefore, they do not have to be quoted.

Wildcard and Regular Expression
The rule engine supports both the wildcard matching operator like and a regular expression matching operator like regex. (It is an operator, not two separate keywords.)

The rule engine supports the * wildcard. For example,

```
"abcd" like "ab*"
```

In case of ambiguity with variable expansion, the * has to be escaped. For example,

```
"abcd" like "a\*d"
```

because "a*d" is interpreted as "a"++str(*d)+"".

When wildcard is not expressive enough, regular expression matching operator can be used. For example,

```
"abcd" like regex "a.c."
```

A regular expression matches the whole string. It follows the syntax of the POSIX API.

Quoting Code
Sometime when you want to pass a string representation of code or regular expressions into an action, it is very tedious to escape every special character in the string. For example,

```
"writeLine(\"stdout\", \*A)"
```

or

```
*A like regex "a\*c\\\\\\[\\]" # matches the regular expression a
    ↪ *c\\\[\]
```

For ease of reading, you can use two backticks ("``") instead of the regular quotes. The rule engine does not further look for variables, etc. in strings between two "``"s. The examples can now be written as:

```
``writeLine("stdout", *A)``
```

and

```
*A like regex ``a*c\\\[\]``
```

5.6.5   DOT EXPRESSION

The dot oeprator provides a simple syntax for creating and accessing key values pair.

To write to a key value pair, use the dot operator on the left-hand side:

```
*A.key = "val"
```

If the key is not a syntactically valid identifier, quotes can be used, escape rules for strings also apply:

```
*A."not␣an␣identifier" = "val"
```

If the variable *A is undefined, a new key value pair data structure will be created.

To read from a key value pair, use the dot operator as binary infix operation in any expression.

Currently key value pairs only support the string type for values.

The str() function is extended to support converting a key value pair data structure to an options format:

```
*A.a="A";
*A.b="B";
*A.c="C";
str(*A); # a=A++++b=B++++c=C
```

5.6.6   CONSTANT

A constant can be defined as a function that returns a constant. A constant defintion has the following syntax:

```
<constant name> = <constant value>
```

where the constant value can be on of the following:

- an integer,

- a double,

- a string (with no variable expansion in it), and

- a Boolean.

A constant name can be used in a pattern and is replaced by its value (whereas a nonconstant is treated as a constructor). For example,

With

```
CONSTANT = 1
```

the following expression

```
match CONSTANT with
   CONSTANT => "CONSTANT"
   *_ => "NOT␣CONSTANT"
```

returns CONSTANT. With a nonconstant function definition such as

```
CONSTANT = time()
```

it returns NOT CONSTANT.

5.6.7   FUNCTION

Function Definition
The rule engine allows defining functions. Functions can be thought of as microservices written in the rule language. The syntax of a function definition is

```
<name>(<param>, ..., <param>) = <expr>
```

For example,

```
square(*n) = *n * *n
```

Function names should be unique (no function-function or function-rule name conflict). Functions can be defined in a mutually exclusive manner. For example,

```
odd(*n) = if *n==0 then false else even(*n-1)
even(*n) = if *n==1 then true else odd(*n-1)
```

Here we cannot use && or || because they do not short circuit like in C or Java.

Calling a Function
To use a function, call it as if it was a microservice.

5.6.8   RULE

Rule Definition
The syntax of a rule with a nontrivial rule condition is as follows:

```
<name>(<param>, ..., <param>) {
  on(<expr>) { <actions> }
}
```

If the rule condition is trivial or unnecessary, the rule can be written in the simpler form:

```
<name>(<param>, ..., <param>) { <actions> }
```

Multiple rules with the same rule name and parameters list can be combined in a more concise syntax where each set of actions is enumerated for each set of conditions:

```
<name>(<param>, ..., <param>) {
  on(<expr>) { <actions> } ...
  on(<expr>) { <actions> }
}
```

Function Name and Rule Name

Function and rule names have to be valid identifiers. Identifiers start with letters followed by letters or digits. For example,

```
ThisIsAValidFunctionNameOrRuleName
```

There should not be whitespaces in a function name or a rule name. For example,

```
This Is Not A Valid Function Name or Rule Name
```

Rule Condition

Rule conditions should be expressions of type `boolean`. The rule is executed only when the rule condition evaluates to true. Which means that there are three failure conditions.

1. Rule condition evaluates to false.

2. Some actions in rule condition fails which causes the evaluation of the whole rule condition to fail.

3. Rule condition evaluates to a value whose type is not Boolean.

For example, if we want to run a rule when the microservice "msi" succeeds, we can write the rule as

```
rule {
  on (msi >= 0) { ... }
}
```

Conversely, if we want to run a rule when the microservice fails, we need to write the rule as

```
rule {
  on (errorcode(msi) < 0) { ... }
}
```

The errormsg microservice captures the error message, allows further processing of the error message, and avoiding the default logging of the error message

```
rule {
  on (errormsg(msi, *msg) < 0 ) { ... }
}
```

By failure condition 3, the following rule condition always fails because msi returns an integer value

```
on(msi) { ... }
```

Generating and Capturing Errors

In a rule, we can also prevent the rule from failing when a microservice fails

```
errorcode(msi)
```

The errormsg microservice captures the error message, allows further processing of the error message, and avoids the default logging of the error message

```
errormsg(msi, *msg)
```

In a rule, the fail and failmsg microservices can be used to generate errors

```
fail(*errorcode)
```

generates an error with an error code

```
failmsg(*errorcode, *errormsg)
```

generates an error with an error code and an error message. For example

```
fail(-1)
failmsg(-1, "this is a user generated error message")
```

The msiExit microservice is similar to failmsg

```
msiExit("-1", "msi")
```

Calling a Rule

To use a rule, call it as if it was a microservice.

5.6.9   DATA TYPES AND PATTERN MATCHING

System Data Types

Lists   A list can be created using the list() microservice. For example,

```
list("This","is","a","list")
```

The elements of a list should have the same type. Elements of a list can be retrieved using the "elem" microservice. The index starts from 0. For example,

```
elem(list("This","is","a","list"),1)
```

evaluates to "is".

If the index is out of range it fails with error code -1.

The `setelem()` takes in three parameters—a list, an index, and a value—and returns a new list that is identical with the list given by the first parameter except that the element at the index given by the second parameter is replace by the value given by the third parameter.

```
setelem(list("This","is","a","list"),1,"isn't")
```

evaluates to

```
list("This","isn't","a","list").
```

If the index is out of range it fails with an error code. The `size` microservice takes in on parameter, a list, and returns the size of the list.

For example,

```
size(list("This","is","a","list"))
```

evaluates to 4.

The `hd()` microservice returns the first element of a list and the `tl()` microservice returns the rest of the list.

If the list is empty then it fails with an error code.

```
hd(list("This","is","a","list"))
```

evaluates to "This" and

```
tl(list("This","is","a","list"))
```

evaluates to

```
list("is","a","list")
```

The `cons()` microservice returns a list by combining an element with another list. For example,

```
cons("This",list("is","a","list"))
```

evaluates to

```
list("This","is","a","list").
```

Tuples   The rule engine supports the built-in data type tuple.

```
( <component>, ..., <component> )
```

Different components may have different types.

Interactions with Packing Instructions   Complex lists such as lists of lists can be constructed locally, but mapping from complex list structures to packing instructions are not yet supported. The supported lists types that can be packed are integer lists and string lists. When remote execute or delay execution is called while there is a complex list in the current runtime environment, an error will be generated. For example, in the following rule

```
test {
    *A = list(list(1,2),list(3,4));
    *B = elem(*A, 1);
    delay("<PLUSET>1m</PLUSET>") {
        writeLine("stdout", *B);
    }
}
```

Even though *A is not used in the delay execution block, the rule will still generate an error. One solution to this is to create a rule with only necessary values.

```
test {
    *A = list(list(1,2),list(3,4));
    *B = elem(*A, 1);
    test(*B);
}
test(*B) {
    delay("<PLUSET>1m</PLUSET>") {
        writeLine("stdout", *B);
    }
}
```

Inductive Data Type

The rule engine allows defining inductive data types. An inductive data type is a data type for values that can be defined inductively, i.e., more complex values can be constructed from simpler values using constructors. The general syntax for inductive data type definition is

```
data <name> [ ( <type parameter list> ) ] =
    | <data constructor name> : <data constructor type>
    . . .
    | <data constructor name> : <data constructor type>
```

For example, a data type that represents the natural numbers can be defined as

```
data nat =
    | zero : nat
    | succ : nat -> nat
```

Here the type name defined is "nat." The type parameter list is empty. If the type parameter list is empty, we may omit it. There are two data constructors. The first constructor "zero" has type "nat," which means that "zero" is a nullary constructor of nat. We use "zero" to represent "0". The second constructor "succ" has type "nat -> nat" which means that "succ" is unary constructor of nat. We use "succ" to represent the successor. With these two constructors we can represent all natural numbers: `zero, succ(zero), succ(succ(zero)), ...` As another example, we can define a data type that represents binary trees of natural numbers

```
data tree =
    | empty : tree
    | node : nat * tree * tree -> tree
```

The `empty` constructor constructs an empty tree, and the `node` constructor takes in a `nat` value, a left subtree, and a right subtree and constructs a tree whose root node value is the "nat" value. The next example shows how to define a polymorphic data type. Suppose that we want to generalize our binary tree data type to those trees whose value type is not "nat." We give the type tree a type parameter X

```
data tree(X) =
    | empty : tree(X)
    | node : X * tree(X) * tree(X) -> tree(X)
```

With a type parameter, `tree` is not a type, but a unary type constructor. A type constructor constructs types from other types. For example, the data type of binary trees of natural numbers is `tree(nat)`. By default, the rule engine parses all types with that starts with uppercase letter as type variables.

Just as data constructors, type constructor can also take multiple parameters. For example,

```
data pair(X, Y) =
    | pair : X * Y -> pair(X, Y)
```

Given the data type definition of "pair," we can construct a pair using "pair" the data constructor. For example,

```
*A = pair(1, 2);
```

Pattern Matching

Pattern Matching In Assignment   Patterns are similar to expressions. For example,

```
pair(*X, *Y)
```

There are a few restrictions. First, only data constructors and free variables may appear in patterns. Second, each variable only occurs once in a pattern (sometimes called linearity). To retrieve the components of *A, we can use patterns on the left hand side of an assignment. For example,

```
pair(*X, *Y) = *A;
```

When this action is executed, *X will be assigned to 1 and *Y will be assigned to 2. Patterns can be combined with let expressions. For example,

```
fib(*n) = if *n==0 then pair(-1, 0)
    else if *n==1 then (0, 1)
    else let pair(*a, *b) = fib(*n - 1) in
        pair(*b, *a + *b)
```

Pseudo Data Constructors   For other types, the rule engine allows the programmer to define pseudo data constructors on them for pattern matching purposes. Pseudo data constructors are like data constructors but can only be used in patterns. Pseudo data constructor definitions are like function definitions except that a pseudo data constructor definition starts with a tilde and must return a tuple. The general syntax is

```
~<name>(<param>) = <expr>
```

A pseudo data constructor can be thought of an inverse function that maps the values in the codomain to values in the domain. For example, we can define the following pseudo data constructor

```
~lowerdigits(*n) = let *a = *n % 10 in ((*n - *a) / 10 % 10, *a)
```

The assignment

```
lowerdigits(*a, *b) = 256;
```

results in *a assigned 5 and *b assigned 6.

5.6.10 CONTROL STRUCTURES

Actions

The iRODS rule engine has a unique concept of recovery action. Every action in a rule definition may have a recovery action. The recovery action is executed when the action fails. This allows iRODS rules to rollback some side effects and restore most of the system state to a previous point. An action recovery block has the form

```
{
    <A1> [ ::: <R1> ]
    <A2> [ ::: <R2> ]
    ...
    <An> [ ::: <Rn> ]
}
```

The basic semantics is that if `Ax` fails then `Rx`, `R(x-1)`, ... `R1` will be executed. The programmer can use this mechanism to restore the system state to the point before this action recovery block is executed.

The rule engine make the distinction between expressions and actions. An expression does not have a recovery action. An action always has a recovery action. If a recovery action is not specified for an action, the rule engine use `nop` as the default recovery action.

Examples of expressions include the rule condition, and the conditional expressions in the `if`, `while`, and `for` actions.

There is no intrinsic difference between an action and an expression. An expression becomes an action when it occurs at an action position in an action recovery block. An action recovery block, in turn, is an expression.

The principle is that an expression should only be used not as an action if it is side-effect free. In the current version, this property is not checked by the rule engine. The programmer has to make sure that it holds for the rule base.

From this perspective, the only difference between functions and rules is nondeterminism.

if

The rule engine has a few useful extensions to the `if` keyword that makes programming in the rule language more convenient.

In addition to the traditional way of using `if`, which will be referred to as the `logical`
↪ `if` where you use if as an action which either succeeds or fails with an error code, the rule engine supports an additional way of using if, which will be referred to as the `functional if`. The `functional if` may return a value of any type if it succeeds. The two different usages have different syntax. The `logical if` has the expected syntax of

```
if <expr> then { <actions> } else { <actions> }
```

while the "functional if" has the following syntax

```
if <expr> then <expr> else <expr>
```

For example, the following are "functional if"s

```
if true then 1 else 0
if *A==1 then true else false
```

To compare, if written in the "logical if" form, the second example would be

```
if (*A==1) then { true; } else { false; }
```

To make the syntax of "logical if" more concise, the rule engine allows the following abbreviation (where the greyed out part can be abbreviated):

```
if (...) then { ... } else { ... }
if (...) then { ... } else { if (...) then {...} else {...} }
```

Multiple abbreviations can be combined for example:

```
if (*X==1) { *A = "Mon"; }
else if (*X==2) {*A = "Tue"; }
else if (*X==3) {*A = "Wed"; }
...
```

foreach

The rule engine allows defining a different variable name for the iterator variables in the foreach action. For example,

```
foreach(*E in *C) {
  writeLine("stdout", *E);
}
```

This is equivalent to

```
foreach(*C) {
  writeLine("stdout", *C);
}
```

This feature allows the collection to be a complex expression. For example,

```
foreach(*E in list("This", "is", "a", "list")) {
  writeLine("stdout", *E);
}
```

This is equivalent to

```
*C = list("This", "is", "a", "list");
foreach(*C) {
    writeLine("stdout", *C);
}
```

The let Expression

As function definitions are based on expressions rather than action sequences, we cannot put an assignment directly inside an expression. For example, the following is not a valid function definition

```
quad(*n) = *t = *n * *n; *t * *t
```

To solve this problem, the let expression provides scoped values in an expression. The general syntax for the let expression is

```
let <assignment> in <expr>
```

For example,

```
quad(*n) = let *t = *n * *n in *t * *t
```

The variable on the left-hand side of the assignment in the let expression is a let-bound variable. The scope of such a variable is within the let expression. A let bound variable should not be reassigned inside the let expression.

The `match` Expression

If a data type has more than one data structure, then the "match" expression is useful

```
match <expr> with
    | <pattern> => <expr>
    ...
    | <pattern> => <expr>
```

For example, given the `nat` data type we defined earlier, we can define the following function using the `match` expression

```
add(*x, *y) =
    match *x with
        | zero => *y
        | succ(*z) => succ(add(*z, *y))
```

For another example, given the "tree" data type we defined earlier, we can define the following function

```
size(*t) =
    match *t with
        | empty => 0
        | node(*v, *l, *r) => 1 + size(*l) + size(*r)
```

5.6.11 RECOVERY CHAIN FOR CONTROL STRUCTURES

Sequence

Syntax:

```
<A1> [ ::: <R1> ]
<A2> [ ::: <R2> ]
...
<An> [ ::: <Rn> ]
```

If Ax fails, then `Rx, ..., R1` are executed

Branch

Syntax:

```
if(<cond>) then {
    <A11> [ ::: <R11> ]
    <A12> [ ::: <R12> ]
    ...
    <A1n> [ ::: <R1n> ]
} else {
    <A21> [ ::: <R21> ]
    <A22> [ ::: <R22> ]
    ...
    <A2n> [ ::: <R2n> ]
} [ ::: R ]
```

If Axy fails, then Rxy, ..., Rx1, R are executed. If cond fails, then R is executed.

Loop

while Syntax:

```
while(<cond>) {
    <A1> [ ::: <R1> ]
    <A2> [ ::: <R2> ]
    ...
    <An> [ ::: <Rn> ]
} [ ::: <R> ]
```

If Ax fails, then Rx, ..., R1, R are executed. If cond fails, then R is executed. Here R should deal with the loop invariant. The recovery chain in the loop restores the loop invariant, and the R restores the machine status from the loop invariant to before the loop is executed.

foreach Syntax:

```
foreach(<var> in <expr>) {
    <A1> [ ::: <R1> ]
    <A2> [ ::: <R2> ]
    ...
    <An> [ ::: <Rn> ]
} [ ::: <R> ]
```

If Ax fails, then Rx, ..., R1, R are executed.

for Syntax:

```
for(<init>; <cond>; <incr>) {
    <A1> [ ::: <R1> ]
    <A2> [ ::: <R2> ]
    ...
    <An> [ ::: <Rn> ]
} [ ::: <R> ]
```

If Ax fails, then Rx, ..., R1, R are executed. If init, cond, or incr fails, then R is executed.

5.6.12 TYPES

Introduction

Types are useful for capturing errors before rules are executed. At the same time, a restrictive type system may also rule out meaningful expressions. As the rule language is a highly dynamic language, the main goal of introducing a type system is the following.

- To enable discovering some errors statically.

- To help remove some repetitive type checking and conversion code in microservices by viewing types as contracts of what kinds of values are passed between the rule engine and microservices.

The type system is designed so that the rule language is dynamically typed when no type information is given, while providing certain static guarantees when some type information is given. The key is combining static typing with dynamic typing, so that we only need to check the statically typed part of a program statically and leave the rest of the program to dynamic typing. The idea is based on Coercion, Soft Typing, and Gradual Typing.

The rule engine uses the central idea of coercion insertion. The rule engine has a fixed coercion relation among its primitive types. Any coercion has to be based on this coercion relation. The coercion relation does not have to be fixed but has to satisfy certain properties. This way, we can potentially adjust the coercion relation without breaking other parts of the type system.

The rule engine distinguishes between two groups of microservices. System provided microservices such as string operators are called internal micro services. The rest are called external microservices. Most internal micro services are statically typed. They come with type information which the type check can make use of to check for errors statically. Currently, all external microservices are dynamically typed.

The rule engine supports a simple form of polymorphism, based on the Hindley-Milner (HM) polymorphism. The idea of HM is that any function type can be polymorphic, but all type variables are universally quantified at the top level. As the rule language does not have higher-order functions, many simplifications can be made. To support certain internal microservices, the type system allows type variables to be bounded, but only to a set of base types.

The type system implemented in the rule engine is an extension to the existing iRODS types by viewing the existing iRODS types as opaque types.

Types
The function parameter and return types can be

```
<btype> ::= boolean
          | integer
          | double
          | string
          | time
          | path
```

```
<stype> ::= <tvar>                    identifiers starting with
    ↪ uppercase letters
          | iRODS types               back quoted string
          | <btype>
          | ?                         dynamic type
          | <stype> * … * <stype>     tuple types
          | c[(<stype>, …, <stype>)]  inductive data types
```

A function type is

```
<ftype> ::= <quanti>, …, <quanti>, <ptype> * <ptype> * … * <
    ↪ ptype> [*|+|?] -> <stype>
```

where

- the <stype> on the right is the return type

- the optional *, +, or ? indicates varargs

- the <ptype> are parameter types of the form

```
<ptype> ::= [(input|output)*|dynamic|actions|expression] [f] <
    ↪ stype>
```

where the optional

- `input` indicates that this is an io parameter

- `output` indicates that this is an output parameter

- `dynamic` indicates that this is an io parameter or output parameter determined dynamically

- `actions` indicates that this is a sequence of actions

- `expression` indicates that this is an expression

- `f` indicates that a coercion can be inserted at compile time based on the coercion relation

  the `<quanti>` are quantifiers of the form

  ```
  <quanti> ::= forall <tvar> [in {<btype> … <btype>}]
  ```

where

- `<tvar>` is a type variable

- the optional set of types provides a bound for the type variable.

Typing Constraint

Type constraints are used in the rule engine to encode typing requirements that need to be checked at compile time or at runtime. The type constraints are solved against a type coercion relation, a model of whether one type can be coerced to another type and how their values should be converted. The type coercion relation can be considered as a directed graph, with types as its vertices, and type coercion functions as its edges.

Types by Examples

For example, binary arithmetic operators such as addition and subtraction are given type:

```
forall X in {integer double}, f X * f X -> X
```

This indicates that the operator takes in two parameters of the same type and returns a value of the same type as its parameters. The parameter type is bounded by {integer double}, which means that the microservice applies to only integers or doubles, but the "f" indicates that if anything can be coerced to these types, they can also be accepted with a runtime conversion inserted. Examples:

(a) double + double => X = double

```
1.0+1.0
```

(b) int + double => X = double

```
1+1.0
```

(c) integer + integer => X = {integer double}

```
1+1
```

(d) unknown + double => X = double Assuming that *A is a fresh variable

```
*A+1.0
```

The type checker generate a constraint that the type of *A can be coerced to double.

(e) unknown + unknown => X = {integer double}

Assuming that *A and *B are fresh variables

```
*A+*B
```

The type checker generate a constraint that the type of *A can be coerced to either integer or double.

Some typing constraints can be solved within certain context. For example, if we put (e) in to the following context:

```
*B = 1.0;
*B = *A + *B;
```

then we can eliminate the possibility that *B is an integer, thereby narrowing the type variable X to double.

Some typing constraints can be proved unsolvable. For example,

```
*B = *A + *B;
*B == "";
```

by the second action we know that *B has to have type string. In this case the rule engine reports a type error.

However, if some typing constraints are not solvable, they are left to be solved at runtime.

Variable Typing

As in C, all variables in the rule language have a fixed type that can not be updated through an assignment. For example, the following does not work:

```
testTyping1 {
    *A = 1;
    *A = "str";
}
```

Once a variable *A is assigned a value X the type of the variable is given by a typing constraint

```
type of X can be coerced to type of *A
```

For brevity, we sometimes denote the "can be coerced to" relation by <=. For example,

```
type of X <= type of *A
```

The reason why the type of *A is not directly assigned to the type of *X is to allow the following usage:

```
testTyping2 {
    *A = 1; # integer <= type of *A
    *A = 2.0; # double <= type of *A
}
```

Otherwise, the programmer would have to write

```
testTyping3 {
    *A = 1.0;
    *A = 2.0;
}
```

to make the rule pass the type checker.

As a more complex example, the following generates a type error:

```
testTyping4 {
    *A = 1; # integer <= type of *A
    if(*A == "str") { # type error
    }
}
```

If the value of a variable is dynamically typed, then a coercion is inserted. The following example works, with a runtime coercion:

```
testTyping2 {
    msi(*A);
    if(*A == "str") { # insert coercion type of *A <= string
    }
}
```

Type Declaration

In the rule engine, you can declare the type of a rule function or a microservice. If the type of an action is declared, then the rule engine will do more static type checking. For example, although

```
concat(*a, *b) = *a ++ *b
add(*a, *b) = concat(*a, *b)
```

does not generate a static type error, add(0, 1) will generate a dynamic type error. This can be solved (generate static type errors instead of dynamic type errors) by declaring the types of the functions

```
concat : string * string -> string
```

```
concat(*a, *b) = *a ++ *b
add : integer * integer -> integer
add(*a, *b) = concat(*a, *b)
```

5.6.13 LANGUAGE INTEGRATED GENERAL QUERY

Language Integrated General Query (LIGQ) provides native syntax support for GenQueries in the rule language and integrates automatic management of thr continuation index and the input and output data structures into the foreach loop. A query expression starts with the key word SELECT and looks exactly the same as a normal GenQuery:

```
SELECT META_DATA_ATTR_NAME WHERE DATA_NAME = 'data_name'
```

At runtime this query is evaluated to an object of type genQueryInp_t * genQueryOut_t. This object can be assigned to a variable:

```
*A = SELECT META_DATA_ATTR_NAME WHERE DATA_NAME = 'data_name';
```

and iterated in a foreach loop:

```
foreach(*Row in *A) {
    ...
}
```

Or we can skip the assignment:

```
foreach(*Row in SELECT META_DATA_ATTR_NAME WHERE DATA_NAME = '
    ↪ data_name' AND COLL_NAME = 'coll_name') {
    ...
}
```

where *Row is a keyValPair_t object that contains the current row in the result set. The break statement can be used to exit the foreach loop.

LIGQ supports the following gen query syntax:

- count, sum, order_desc, order_asc

- =, <>, >, <, >=, <=, in, between, like, not like

- || and &&

LIGQ also provides support for using == and != as equality predicates, in order to be consistent with the rule engine syntax.

The left-hand side of comparison operators is always a column name, but the right-hand side of a comparison operator is always one (or more in the case of between) normal Rule Engine expression(s) which is(are) evaluated by the rule engine first. Therefore, we can use any rule engine expression on the right-hand side of a comparison operator. If the right-hand side operand is not a simple single quoted string or number, then the LIGQ query cannot be executed from the iquery command.

One potential confusion is that the `like` and `not like` operators in the gen query syntax differ from those in the Rule Language. The right-hand side operand is first evaluated by the rule engine to a string which in turn is interpreted by the qen query subsystem. Therefore, LIGQ queries do not use the same syntax for wildcards as the rule engine (unless the wildcards are in a nested rule engine expression). While the rule engine uses * for wildcards, qen query uses the standard SQL syntax for wildcards.

5.6.14 PATH LITERALS

A path literal starts with a slash:

```
/tempZone/home/rods
```

A path literal is just like a string, you can use variable expansion, escape characters, etc.:

```
/*Zone/home/*User/\\.txt
```

In addition to the characters that must be escaped in a string, the following characters must also be escaped in a path literal:

```
','    comma
';'    semicolon
')'    right parenthesis
'␣'    space
```

A path literal can be assigned to a variable:

```
*H = /tempZone/home/rods
```

New path literals can be constructed from paths but it must start with "/", the rule engine automatically removes redundant leading slashes in a path:

```
*F = /*H/foo.txt
```

Path literals can be used in various places. If a path literal points to a collection, it can be used in a foreach loop to loop over all data objects under that collection.

```
foreach(*D in *H) {
   ...
}
```

A path literal can also be used in collection and data object-related microservice calls:

```
msiCollCreate(/*H/newColl, "", *Status);
msiRmColl(/*H/newColl, "", *Status);
```

5.7   DELAY EXECUTION

Rules can be run one of three ways:

- manually, via irule;

- triggered, via Policy Enforcement Points (PEPs); or

- periodically, via delayed execution.

Most of the actions and microservices executed by the rule engine are executed manually or via PEPs, however, some actions are better suited to be placed in a queue and executed later. The actions and microservices which are to be executed in delay mode can be queued with the `delay` microservice.

Typically, delayed actions and microservices are resource-heavy, time-intensive processes, better suited to being carried out without having the user wait for their completion. These delayed processes can also be used for cleanup and general maintenance of the iRODS system, like the `cron` in UNIX.

Monitoring the delayed queue is important once your workflows and maintenance scripts depend on the health of the system. The delayed queue can be managed with the following three iCommands:

1. iqstat — show the queue status of delayed rules.

2. iqmod — modify certain values in existing delayed rules (owned by you).

3. iqdel — remove a delayed rule (owned by you) from the queue.

5.7.1   SYNTAX

The `delay` microservice is invoked with the following syntax:

```
delay("hints") {
        microservice-chain_part1;
        microservice-chain_part2;
        microservice-chain_part3;

        .

        .

        .

        microservice-chain_partN;
  }
```

hints (required) are of the form:

- ET - Execution Time — Absolute time (without time zones) when the delayed execution should be performed. The input can be incremental time given in:

- – nnnn — an integer - assumed to be in seconds

- – nnnnU — nnnn is an integer, U is the unit (s-seconds, m-minutes, h-hours, d-days, y-years)

- – dd.hh:mm:ss — 2-digit integers representing days, hours, minutes, and seconds, respectively. Most significant values can be omitted (e.g., 20:40 means mm:ss)

- – YYYY-MM-DD.hh:mm:ss — Least significant values can be omitted (e.g., 2015-07-29.12 means noon of July 29, 2015)

- PLUSET - Relative Execution Time — Relative to current time when the delayed execution should be performed.

- EF - Execution Frequency — How often the delayed execution should be performed. The EF value is of the form:

  - – nnnnU <directive> where

    * nnnn is an integer, U is the unit (s-seconds, m-minutes, h-hours, d-days, y-years)
    * <directive> can be of the form:
      · <empty-directive> - equivalent to REPEAT FOR EVER
      · REPEAT FOR EVER
      · REPEAT UNTIL SUCCESS
      · REPEAT nnnn TIMES - nnnn is an integer
      · REPEAT UNTIL <time> - <time> is of the form YYYY-MM-DD.hh:mm:ss
      · REPEAT UNTIL SUCCESS OR UNTIL <time>
      · REPEAT UNTIL SUCCESS OR nnnn TIMES
      · DOUBLE FOR EVER
      · DOUBLE UNTIL SUCCESS
      · DOUBLE nnnn TIMES
      · DOUBLE UNTIL <time>
      · DOUBLE UNTIL SUCCESS OR UNTIL <time>
      · DOUBLE UNTIL SUCCESS OR nnnn TIMES

5.7.2   EXAMPLES

This example will queue the chain of microservices to begin in 1 minute and repeat every 20 minutes forever:

```
delay("<PLUSET>1m</PLUSET><EF>20m</EF>") {
    writeLine("serverLog", " -- Delayed Execution");
}
```

5.8   REMOTE EXECUTION

A microservice chain can be executed on a remote iRODS server. This gives the flexibility to "park" microservices where it is most optimal. For example, if there is a microservice which needs considerable computational power, then performing it at a compute-intensive site would be appropriate. Similarly, if one is computing checksums, performing it at the server where the data is located would be more appropriate.

5.8.1   SYNTAX

The `remote` microservice is invoked with the following syntax:

```
remote("host","hints") {
        microservice-chain_part1;
        microservice-chain_part2;
        microservice-chain_part3;
        .
        .
        .
        microservice-chain_partN;
    }
```

host (required) is the hostname on which the remote execution should be performed.
hints (required) are of the form:

- ZONE - Remote Zone — The name of the Zone in which the `host` is located.

5.8.2   EXAMPLES

This example will execute the chain of microservices on the host `resource.example.org` in the local Zone:

```
remote("resource.example.org","") {
    writeLine("serverLog", " -- Remote Execution in Local Zone");
}
```

This example will execute the chain of microservices on the host `farawayicat.example.`
↪ `org` in the remote Zone named `DifferentZone`:

```
remote("farawayicat.example.org","<ZONE>DifferentZone</ZONE>") {
    writeLine("serverLog", " -- Remote Zone Execution");
}
```

The best practice for using both `delay()` and `remote()` depends on the use case.

CHAPTER 6

iRODS Microservices

Microservices are small, well-defined procedures/functions that perform a simple task. Microservices are developed and made available by system programmers and application programmers and compiled into the iRODS Server code. Users and administrators can chain these microservices to implement a function that they want to use or provide for others. In this manner, the users/administrators can have full control over what happens when one performs a macro-level functionality. These macro-level functionalities are called Actions. By having more than one chain of Microservices for an Action, a system can have multiple ways of performing the Action. Using priorities and validation conditions at run-time, the system chooses the "best" microservice chain to be executed. There are other caveats to this execution paradigm that were discussed in Chapter 4.

The task performed by a microservice can be quite small or very involved. We leave it to the microservice developer to choose the proper level of granularity for their task differentiation. A good rule of thumb is to divide a large task into subtasks with well-defined interfaces and make each into a microservice. If two such subtasks are always done together, it would be a good idea to group them together into one microservice. Since the user/administrator chains the microservices into Actions, having too fine-grained a differentiation will make the splicing cumbersome and difficult. On the other hand, making a large task into a single microservice takes away the control that is given to the end user/administrator, who might want to choose not to do some parts of the task. We recommend that normal coding practices and good design principles used in Module and method generation be applied in deciding the granularity for each microservice task.

The microservices are organized into the following categories.

- Core microservices—Functions for Rule Engine control, Workflow creation, Data Object Low-level manipulation, Higher-level Data Object.

- iCAT Services—Functions for manipulating System metadata, and for interacting with the iCAT Metadata Catalog.

- Framework Services—Functions for Rule-Oriented remote database access, high-performance message passing, sending e-mail, manipulating Keyword—Value attribute pairs, supporting User-defined services, and supporting System level services.

- Module microservices—Sets of functions developed for specific communities, for example, the ERA (Electronic Records Archives) Program at NARA, eXtensible Markup Language

(XML) manipulation, Hierarchical Data Format (HDF) manipulation, image property manipulation, Web service interaction, the French National Library, etc.

Within each category, multiple microservices may be defined. The list continues to grow over time as more functionality is added to the iRODS Data Grid.

The microservices for the low-level manipulation of data objects correspond to standard Posix I/O operations. A file can be opened, read or written, and closed. For partial reads on a file, an Lseek can be done to the correct location within the file.

Higher-level data and collection operations correspond to manipulation of objects (files). A file can be put into the iRODS Data Grid (msiDataObjPut microservice), or read from the Data Grid (msiDataObjGet microservice). A file can be copied between subcollections (msiDataObjCopy). Or it can be physically moved to another storage location (msiDataObjPhymv). A file can be replicated (msiDataObjRepl). In this case, an additional physical copy is made. A file in a remote storage location can be registered into the data grid (msiPhyPathReg). Operations on files include setting access controls, creating checksums, renaming, and deleting. Deletion of a file corresponds to a logical move into a trashcan collection. Collections can be created, replicated, and deleted.

The microservices provided by iRODS are written in C and installed with the iRODS Server at each storage location. This makes it possible to tightly control the functions that are executed at each storage location, and ensure a consistent operation. In addition, iRODS supports the invocation of remote commands to run applications that have been installed outside of iRODS at the remote storage location.

The iRODS Data Grid can issue commands against a remote database. Currently, the remote database is assumed to be the same as the database that holds the iCAT Metadata Catalog. The operations that can be performed on the remote database include execution of SQL operations, updates to metadata, and formatting of results. The result of the operation can be ignored (not returned), or written to standardout, or written into an iRODS data object.

The iRODS Data Grid can send messages through e-mail. A message can be composed and sent, or the information that has been written to the REI standardout structure can be sent.

Metadata can be added to iRODS individually, or loaded into an iRODS Data Grid in batches, by constructing a file that lists keyword—value—unit triplets. For each keyword name, the value and unit are specified, along with the file name to which the attributes will be assigned. A structure in memory holds the information when queries are made on the iCAT catalog. microservices are provided to extract the value from the memory structure, write the values to standardout, ingest the metadata into the iCAT catalog, and remove attributes from the iCAT catalog. The format of the keyword—value pairs can be converted into "%" delimited strings.

User-level microservices support interactive use of the iRODS Data Grid. The types of functions range from retrieval and formatting of the system time, to loading metadata from a file, to writing a buffer to standardout, to writing an integer to standardout.

The iRODS Data Grid has system level microservices that can only be called by the server process. These microservices cannot be invoked using the interactive "irule" command. The functions that are supported include setting access controls, turning off the ability to delete files, setting the default location where data will be written, specifying the number of parallel I/O streams to be used for transferring large files, and restricting the operations that can be executed by a "public" user.

The NARA Transcontinental Persistent Archive Prototype uses microservices to manipulate the hierarchical metadata associated with the Life Cycle Data Requirements Guide, parse audit trails, extract and load lists of access controls, extract and load user-defined metadata, and replicate collections. These functions are needed to implement trusted repository assessment criteria.

The iRODS Data Grid can apply an Extensible Stylesheet Language Transformation (XSLT) to an XML file, and store the resulting file in the iRODS Data Grid.

HDF is used to package scientific data into containers (files). HDF libraries are invoked by the iRODS server at the remote storage location to extract files from the HDF container, read data from a file, and read data attributes.

Images contain metadata that describe the type of image, how the image was created, and the properties of the image. In order to manipulate an image, the properties are extracted from the image. A generic set of microservices has been developed to support manipulation of a set of properties.

The French National Library created a microservice to format the system time.

Although microservices can be any normal C procedure, there is a standard template that needs to be used when making a C procedure into a microservice. The standard template provides the in-memory structures that are used to pass data between microservices, a mechanism to check interactions between microservices, and standard error returns. A C procedure that you want to turn into a microservice can have any number of arguments and any type or structure (with some caveats, see discussion on the parameter structure). When the Rule Engine interacts with a Microservice, it interacts with a published (standardized within iRODS) parametric structure of the type called msParam_t. Hence, glue code is needed that converts from msParam_t to the actual argument types of the underlying microservice. We call this glue code a microservice interface (msi for short). The msi routine will map the msParam_t structure to the call arguments and convert back any output parameters to the msParam_t structure. We illustrate with an example below.

We recommend that the microservice interface procedures be pre-fixed with the three-letter acronym msi. Hence, a procedure called createCollection can have an interface routine called msiCreateCollection. The Rule Engine will invoke msiCreateCollection that, in turn, will invoke createCollection.

Each of the msi procedure calls is registered in the Rule Engine. Only these registered microservices can be invoked by the Rule Engine. The iRODS Data Grid supports the organization of microservices into plugins. The iRODS Data Grid administrator specifies which plugins will be loaded at each iRODS Server.

6.1   MICROSERVICE INPUT/OUTPUT ARGUMENTS

One can pass arguments to a Rule, microservice, or Action through explicit arguments, as done in the case of C function or procedure calls. The input parameters can take two forms.

- **Variable**—If an argument begins with the * character, it is treated as a variable argument. Variable arguments can be used both as input and output parameters. The output parameter from one microservice can be explicitly specified as the input parameter of another microservice. This powerful capability allows very complex workflow-like Rules to be constructed. For example, in the following workflow chain.

- **Expression**—The argument can also be any valid iRODS Rule Language expression. The expression is evaluated to a value at runtime. For example, in the microservice msiSetRescSortScheme ("random"), the character string "random" will be passed in as input. Expressions can only be used as input parameters and not output parameters.

  For example, in

```
msiDataObjOpen("/x/y/z",*FD);
msiDataObjRead(*FD,10000,*BUF);
```

  msiDataObjOpen opens a data object with the input path /x/y/z and the output file descriptor is placed in the variable parameter *FD. *FD is then used by msiDataObjRead as an input parameter for the read.

  User-level workflow-like Rules can be invoked through the irule command or the rcExecMyRule API. Internally, the Rule system uses the msParam_t structure to store the content of Variable arguments. The definition of the structure can be found in the file lib/api/include/dataObjInpOut.h.

6.2   ABOUT MICROSERVICES AND MICROSERVICE PLUGINS

An iRODS microservice is a C function which takes as parameters:

- one argument of type ruleExecInfo_t* (required) and

- any number of arguments of type msParam_t* (optional).

  Input and output values of a microservice are passed through its msParam_t* arguments.

```
typedef struct MsParam {
  char *label;
```

```
char *type; /* this is the name of the packing instruction in
    ↪ rodsPackTable.h */
void *inOutStruct;
bytesBuf_t *inpOutBuf;
} msParam_t;
```

This data structure is universal in the sense that it can be used to represent all parameter types, including very complex data structures. The field label is the identifier used in the actual Rule. That is, if a Rule calls the microservice msiDataObjCreate(*A,*S_FD), the strings *A and *S_FD are the labels of their respective structures. The type field identifies the type of data that is stored in the inOutStruct. The data types supported, although fairly extensive, are restricted to the ones that are given in the file lib/core/include/rodsDef.h. The value of I/O is specified in the inOutStruct field. The inpOutBuf is a buffer that can be used to pass binary data as part of the parameter. The parameters are passed as an array as defined in the following type definition.

The msParam_t structure provides a uniform type definition for the Rule Engine to handle and operate. The data structures include support for passing parameters for Rule invocation using the msParam structure and for passing values between client—server and server—server interactions. The values can be found in the file lib/core/include/rodsPackTable.h.

The inOutStruct tells the iRODS Data Grid where the value defined by the input structure is located. The inOutStuct is a pointer to the value of the input structure being passed. It can be null. The inpOutBuf is used to hold any binary buffers that need to be passed as part of the argument.

A set of helper functions is commonly used in microservices to interface with the generic msParam_t* type:

- parseMspForXxx() for inputs

- fillXxxInMsParam() for outputs

where Xxx varies depending on the type of parameter (Str, Int, DataObjInp, etc.).

iRODS allows microservices to be dynamically loaded as plugins, without the need to re-build the iRODS server.

6.3 EXAMPLES

The following examples come from the 'irods_training' online code repository. You can clone them to your local machine with 'git clone https://github.com/irods/irods_training'.

The example code below can be found at:

```
~/irods_training/advanced/irods_microservice_plugin/src/lib-
    ↪ microservice-example.cpp
```

6.3.1 THE PLUGIN FACTORY

The Plugin Factory has the following components:

```
extern "C"
irods::ms_table_entry* plugin_factory() {
    ...
      return msvc;
}
```

It must have C linkage, must return an `irods::plugin_base` derived type, and must be named `plugin_factory`. In the function, it first instantiates a microservice plugin:

```
irods::ms_table_entry* msvc = new irods::ms_table_entry(3);
```

It allocates a raw pointer to `irods::ms_table_entry`, passes its constructor the number of parameters *not including the ruleExecInfo_t**. Second, it wires a plugin operation:

```
msvc->add_operation<
  msParam_t*,
    msParam_t*,
    msParam_t*,
    ruleExecInfo_t*>(
      "msiexample_microservice",
       std::function<int(
         msParam_t*,
           msParam_t*,
           msParam_t*,
           ruleExecInfo_t*)>(msiexample_microservice));
```

Template parameters are the parameters of the function operation. The first parameter is the calling name of the operation - `msiexample_microservice`. The second parameter is a `std ↪ ::function` wrapping the local function definition, which takes the full signature of the function as a template parameter and takes the function pointer as an argument. To put them together,

```
  extern "C"
  irods::ms_table_entry* plugin_factory() {
      irods::ms_table_entry* msvc = new irods::ms_table_entry
          ↪ (3);
      msvc->add_operation<
      msParam_t*,
      msParam_t*,
      msParam_t*,
      ruleExecInfo_t*>(
```

```
        "msiexample_microservice",
            std::function<int(
          msParam_t*,
           msParam_t*,
           msParam_t*,
           ruleExecInfo_t*)>(msiexample_microservice));
       return msvc;
  }
```

6.3.2   THE MICROSERVICE DEFINITION

The signature is

```
int msiexample_microservice(
      msParam_t*            _string_param,
      msParam_t*            _int_param,
      msParam_t*            _double_param,
      ruleExecInfo_t* _rei ) {
    ...
      return 0;
}
```

It returns an int, takes N (per the constructor) number of msParam_t*, and must end in a ruleExecInfo_t*. In the function, it first does parameter parsing and error Checking

```
char *string_param = parseMspForStr( _string_param );
if( !string_param ) {
      std::cout << "null _string_param" << std::endl;
      return SYS_INVALID_INPUT_PARAM;
}

int int_param = parseMspForPosInt( _int_param );
if( int_param < 0 ) {
      std::cout << "invalid _int_param" << std::endl;
      return SYS_INVALID_INPUT_PARAM;
}

double double_param = 0.0;
int ret = parseMspForDouble( _double_param, &double_param );
if( ret < 0 ) {
      std::cout << "invalid _double_param" << std::endl;
      return SYS_INVALID_INPUT_PARAM;
```

```
}
```

msParam_t* must be parsed into native types. Individual parseMspFor* exist for most iRODS types. Either the type is returned, if possible—or an error code is returned. After that, you can add application code. In this example, we just write a string to the server log.

```
std::cout << __FUNCTION__
        << " string [" << string_param
        << "] int [" << int_param
        << "] double [" << double_param
        << "]" << std::endl;
```

To put them together,

```
int msiexample_microservice(
        msParam_t*          _string_param,
        msParam_t*          _int_param,
        msParam_t*          _double_param,
        ruleExecInfo_t* _rei ) {

        char *string_param = parseMspForStr( _string_param );
        if( !string_param ) {
                std::cout << "null _string_param" << std::endl;
                return SYS_INVALID_INPUT_PARAM;
        }

        int int_param = parseMspForPosInt( _int_param );
        if( int_param < 0 ) {
                std::cout << "invalid _int_param" << std::endl;
                return SYS_INVALID_INPUT_PARAM;
        }

        double double_param = 0.0;
        int ret = parseMspForDouble( _double_param, &double_param
          ↪ );
        if( ret < 0 ) {
                std::cout << "invalid _double_param" << std::endl;
                return SYS_INVALID_INPUT_PARAM;
        }
```

```
    std::cout << __FUNCTION__ << " string [" << string_param
        ↪ << "] int [" << int_param << "] double [" <<
        ↪ double_param << "]" << std::endl;

    return 0;
}
```

Many things are possible in a microservice, such as calling server-side API endpoints, for example, rsGenQuery, or manipulating data at rest.

6.3.3   BUILDING AND INSTALLING THE EXAMPLE CODE

Having already installed the apt repository located at https://packages.irods.org, the following steps will install the buildchain and prerequisites for building the example microservice.

```
$ sudo apt-get -y install irods-externals-*

$ export PATH=/opt/irods-externals/cmake3.5.2-0/bin:$PATH

$ which cmake /opt/irods-externals/cmake3.5.2-0/bin/cmake

$ sudo apt-get install irods-dev
```

Then, we build the example package and install it with:

```
$ cd ~/build_msvc

$ cmake ~/irods_training/advanced/irods_microservice_plugin

$ make package

$ sudo dpkg -i irods-microservice-example-4.2.0-ubuntu14-x86_64.
    ↪ deb
```

6.3.4   TESTING THE MICROSERVICE

We create a rule to test the microservice. We edit the /etc/irods/training.re rulebase.

```
acPostProcForPut() {

    microservice_example("XXXX - test string", 314, 123.4);

    if("ufs_cache" == $KVPairs.rescName ) {
```

```
        writeLine( "serverLog", "XXXX - calling delayed
            ↪ replication" );
        delay("<PLUSET>1s</PLUSET><EF>1h DOUBLE UNTIL SUCCESS OR
            ↪ 6 TIMES</EF>") {
          *CacheRescName = "comp_resc;ufs_cache";
          msisync_to_archive("*CacheRescName", $filePath,
              ↪ $objPath );
        }
    }
}
```

Now we can test the microservice.

```
iput VERSION.json
```

```
grep -dskip ``XXXX -'' ./log/*
```

should see in the log:

```
./log/rodsLog.2016.06.XX:msiexample_microservice string [XXXX -
    ↪ test string] int [314] double [123.4]
```

APPENDIX A

Exercises

A student that takes a class on policy-based data management should be able to answer the following questions about the iRODS Data Grid. They are divided into short factual questions and longer essay-style questions.

A.1 SHORT QUESTIONS

- Explain what `core.re` is and what role it plays within an implementation of iRODS.

- Explain what the **iCAT** is and what role it plays within an implementation of iRODS.

- For a given rule, identify **two** different ways that you could invoke the rule (i.e., make the rule run within iRODS). For each of these two ways to invoke the rule, provide one reason why you might decide to choose it over the other way.

- Identify the software that needs to be installed on your computer in order to run an iRODS client.

- Identify the software that needs to be installed on your computer in order to run a complete iRODS Data Grid.

- Briefly explain the relationship between: (1) a policy and a rule and (2) a rule and microservice.

- List the **four** main parts of an iRODS rule. Provide an example an actual iRODS rule that includes all four of these parts.

- Identify and briefly explain **three** different types of events that can trigger an iRODS rule.

- Provide a human language explanation of a **condition** that you could specify in a rule.

- Provide a human language explanation of a **recovery action** that you could specify in a rule.

- Identify **three** different ways in which interactions between independent data grids can be **federated**.

- Identify **two** different iRODS clients and briefly explain **one** potential advantage and **one** potential disadvantage of using each as a way to access an iRODS Data Grid.

- Identify **two** iCommands and briefly explain what each one does.

- Identify **two** system microservices and briefly explain what each one does.

- Explain what a whiteboard variable is and provide **two** examples.

- Explain the purpose of the `delay` microservice and provide **one** example (either using iRODS Rule Language syntax or explained in human language) of how `delay` could be used.

- Explain the purpose of the `foreach` microservice and provide **one** example (either using iRODS Rule Language syntax or explained in human language) of how `foreach` could be used.

- Explain the purpose of the `writeLine` microservice and provide one example (either using iRODS Rule Language syntax or explained in human language) of how `writeLine` could be used.

- Explain what `nop` means when it is included in an iRODS rule.

- Identify **one** command and **two** microservices that can be used to query iCAT. Briefly explain the main differences between these three approaches.

- Provide **two** examples (either using iRODS Rule Language syntax or explained in human language) of actions that a repository might want to carry out each time the `acCreateUser` microservice is executed.

- Identify the **three** main parts of an `irule` inputFile and provide **one** example for each part.

- Explain what a Persistent State Variable is and provide **two** examples.

- Explain why there are two different syntaxes for writing rules in iRODS and identify a way to translate from the more human-readable to the more compact version.

- Explain **two** different ways to change the `core.re` file.

- Explain **one** way in which the iRODS Rule Language is particularly sensitive to small differences in what you type into the rule and provide **one** example (either using iRODS Rule Language syntax or explained in human language) of how this sensitivity could cause you trouble when trying execute a rule.

A.2   ESSAY QUESTIONS

- Explain what a data grid is and the key capabilities of the iRODS Data Grid system. Explain how a scientific research project might use an iRODS Data Grid. Explain how a library might use an iRODS Data Grid. Explain how an archive might use an iRODS Data Grid.

- Draw a diagram of an iRODS Data Grid and explain the architecture.

- Explain the main challenges of sharing distributed data and how iRODS approaches this.

- Explain the main challenges of managing large-scale distributed digital data and how iRODS approaches this.

- Explain the main challenges of preserving digital data and how iRODS approaches this.

- Identify and explain something about iRODS that could be **improved**. Be specific about (1) what the problem is, (2) why you see it as a problem, and (3) how it could be fixed (not a detailed proposal for how to implement the fix, but just an explanation of what could be done to fix it).

- Identify and explain what you see as the **three** most important **challenges** to an institution that would like to implement iRODS. Be specific about (1) what the challenges are and why you think they are important.

- Your institution has installed DSpace and is using it to manage various digital collections. Your boss has been told that she should also consider implementing iRODS. She is a very thoughtful and responsible administrator but is not familiar with iRODS, data grids, or the mechanics of programming. She has asked you to explain to her why iRODS would be worth considering, given that DSpace is already up and running successfully. Provide **two** reasons why she might want to consider iRODS. For each reason, provide an explanation and an example to illustrate your point. (Note: You should assume that your institution is successfully applying the existing features of DSpace, so your answer should focus on core capabilities of the software, rather than the usability of DSpace.)

- Identify one of the criteria from the Trustworthy Repositories Audit & Certification: Criteria and Checklist (TRAC). Provide human language (i.e., not in iRODS syntax) description of (1) a rule that could be used to meet that criterion and (2) how you could determine whether the rule had done what you intended it to do.

- iRODS is designed to support "data virtualization." Explain what this means and why it is desirable. In your answer, provide **three** examples of data virtualization within iRODS.

- iRODS is designed to support "policy virtualization." Explain what this means and why it is desirable in general. Then use **one** specific example of a policy being "virtualized" in iRODS and **two** specific reasons why policy virtualization would be beneficial in this case.

- Identify and explain **three** characteristics of a policy that increase the chances that someone will be able to write iRODS rules to enforce the policy.

- Explain the differences between atomic, deferred, and periodic rules. Provide **one** example (either using iRODS Rule Language syntax or explained in human language) of each. Describe **two** different cases in which delayed execution of a rule (or set of rules) would be desirable, and describe **two** different cases in which delayed execution of a rule (or set of rules) would be undesirable.

Authors' Biographies

HAO XU

Hao Xu is a research scientist at the Data Intensive Cyber Environment Center, University of North Carolina at Chapel Hill. He has been working on improving the rule engine and the rule language, and the metadata catalog of the integrated Rule-Oriented Data System (iRODS) since 2010. He developed pluggable rule engine architecture that allows interoperability between different programming languages and the iRODS data management systems. He also developed QueryArrow, a semantically unified query and update system that allows bidirectional integration of metadata from multiple heterogeneous data stores. His research interests include theory of data management, automatic theorem proving, programming languages, distributed data systems, and formal methods in software development. He has a B.E. in computer science and engineering and a B.S. minor in applied mathematics from Beihang University and a Ph.D. in computer science from University of North Carolina at Chapel Hill.

TERRELL RUSSELL

Terrell Russell is serving as the Chief Technologist of the iRODS Consortium at the Renaissance Computing Institute (RENCI). Terrell works on build and test for iRODS as well as code review, package management, documentation, and high-level architecture design. He's interested in distributed systems, metadata, security, and open source software that accelerates science. Terrell holds a B.S. in computer engineering, a B.S. in information technology and service organizations, an M.S. in computer networking from North Carolina State University, and a Ph.D. in information science from the University of North Carolina at Chapel Hill. Terrell has been working on iRODS since 2008.

JASON COPOSKY

Jason Coposky is the Executive Director of the iRODS Consortium at the Renaissance Computing Institute (RENCI). With over 20 years of industry experience, Jason has worked in a variety of areas including virtual reality, EDA, visualization, and data management. Prior to RENCI, Jason was Technical Director for a startup where he developed projection and distortion correction technologies. During his tenure at RENCI, he began as the first member of the Visualization team, creating novel large format display and multitouch systems. He then moved to the irods@renci project as technical lead where he later became Chief Technologist of the iRODS Consortium. In his current role, he provides management oversight for the entire Consortium.

ARCOT RAJASEKAR

Arcot Rajasekar is a professor in the School of Library and Information Sciences at the University of North Carolina, Chapel Hill, and a chief scientist at the Renaissance Computing Institute (RENCI). Previously, he was at the San Diego Supercomputer Center at the University of California, San Diego, leading the Data Grids Technology Group. He has been involved in research and development of data grid middleware systems for over a decade and is a lead originator behind the concepts in the Storage Resource Broker (SRB) and the integrated Rule Oriented Data Systems (iRODS), two premier data grid middleware developed by the Data Intensive Cyber Environments Group. Dr. Rajasekar has a Ph.D. in computer science from the University of Maryland at College Park and has more than 100 publications in the areas of data grids, logic programming, deductive databases, digital library, and persistent archives.

REAGAN MOORE

Reagan Moore (retired) was a professor in the School of Information and Library Science at the University of North Carolina, Chapel Hill, chief scientist for Data Intensive Cyber Environments at the Renaissance Computing Institute, and director of the Data Intensive Cyber Environments Center at University of North Carolina. He coordinates research efforts in development of data grids, digital libraries, and preservation environments. Developed software systems include the Storage Resource Broker data grid and the integrated Rule-Oriented Data System. Supported projects include the National Archives and Records Administration Transcontinental Persistent Archive Prototype, and science data grids for seismology, oceanography, climate, high-energy physics, astronomy, and bioinformatics. An ongoing research interest is use of data grid technology to automate execution of management policies and validate trustworthiness of repositories. Dr. Moore's previous roles include the following: director of the DICE group at the San Diego Supercomputer Center, and manager of production services at SDSC. He previously worked as a computational plasma physicist at General Atomics on equilibrium and stability of toroidal fusion devices. He has a Ph.D. in plasma physics from the University of California, San Diego (1978), and a B.S. in physics from the California Institute of Technology (1967).

ANTOINE DE TORCY

Antoine de Torcy is a developer with the iRODS Consortium. He worked with the DICE group since 2003, at the University of California, San Diego, until 2008, and now at the University of North Carolina, Chapel Hill. Antoine has implemented client interfaces for SRB and server modules for iRODS. His technical expertise has helped various groups build preservation environments based on iRODS and focused on data and metadata. Antoine holds an engineering degree in applied mathematics and computer science from the University of Paris–Dauphine.

MICHAEL WAN

Michael Wan (retired) led the Data Intensive Cyber Environment (DICE) group of Institute of Neural Science (INC) at University of California, San Diego. He is the chief software architect of the Integrated Rule-Oriented Data System (iRODS) and the Storage Resource Broker (SRB). Before SRB, Michael spent 10 years developing operating systems and archival storage systems at SDSC. Michael received his B.S. degree from Illinois State University and M.S. from Georgia Institute of Technology.

WAYNE SCHROEDER

Wayne Schroeder (retired) was a senior software engineer with the iRODS team and, with Dr. Arcot Rajasekar and Michael Wan, designed and developed the core iRODS system. His contributions include the database catalog interface, administration tools, metadata interfaces, security/authentication, and installation and testing subsystems. He has over 30 years of experience in software engineering, with expertise in data management, computer security, networking, scientific applications, high-performance computing, and system support/administration. He earned a B.S. in computer science in 1976, magna cum laude, with a minor in psychology.

SHEAU-YEN CHEN

Sheau-Yen Chen (retired) was the Data Intensive Cyber Environment (DICE) Center's Data Grid System Administrator for iRODS. Before DICE, she was with San Diego Supercomputer Center (SDSC) as a programmer/analyst and administered the Storage Resource Broker (SRB). She gained valuable experience as SRB system administrator since 2001. Before moving to California, she worked with Solucient (company that produced 100 top hospitals), University of Michigan's Department of Radiology, Motoresearch, Northern Telecom, and Dictaphone R&D Center as computer programmer/analyst. Sheau-Yen has an M.S. degree in biostatistics from Virginia Commonwealth University and another M.S. degree in mathematics from Virginia State University.

Printed in the United States
by Baker & Taylor Publisher Services